APPALACHIA
POPULAR BELIEFS
The Devil has a Pretty Face

Theresa C. Gaynord

TRANSCENDENT ZERO PRESS
HOUSTON, TEXAS

Cover design: Nathan P. Khanna

Publisher contact: Editor@transcendentzeropress.org

ISBN: 978-1-946460-74-5

APPALACHIA

POPULAR BELIEFS

The Devil has a Pretty Face

Theresa C. Gaynord

TABLE OF CONTENTS

THE RIVER'S SONG / 7

RESOUND / 14

LOW MURMURS / 19

FLOOD AND FOWL / 23

DISSOLUTION / 26

BREED / 28

IDOLATRY / 30

PRIMAL BLOOD / 34

MARRIAGE / 36

THE DARKSOME STATESMAN / 40

CONDEMNING THOUGHTS / 44

MIDNIGHT-FOG / 47

WEIGHTS AND WOE / 49

PURSUED / 51

GNATS AND FLIES / 53

ANCIENTS / 54

PRECEDENT TO PLEAD / 57

CRYPTIC / 58

DISTANT WOODS / 60

UPON THE DISTANT WATERS / 62

PEEPING AT MORN / 64

A CIRCLE DIVIDED / 67

DISTURBED SLOPES OF HILLS / 69

BORN OF CHAINS AND MOODS / 71

SOLITUDE / 73

THE TANGLED MASS OF WILL AND FATE / 77

THE DEBATABLE SOUL / 79

SWEET ASSURANCES / 81

A WEARY CIRCUIT / 85

WARNING SIGNS / 86

WHITE ROSES / 87

FALCONS SNARED / 91

WARRIOR HORSES / 93

A BEETLE'S PASS / 95

NECTAR / 97

PURPLE / 99

DEAD DREAMS-FORSAKEN DAYS / 101

PROPHECY / 102

TIME'S TRAGEDY / 103

DISTORTED / 104

IMMORTALITY / 106

SHAPESHIFTER / 108

VIBRATIONS / 109

DEATHLESS MUSIC / 113

BLACK RAIN / 115

HUMAN SLEEP / 116

THE WATCHMAN / 117

INTERRUPTED CRY / 119

SACRIFICE / 121

DOMINION / 123

TEARS AND SEPULCHRE / 125

BOUNTY FOR THE DECEASED / 131

Prologue: The River's Song

The river runs black, a vein of ink through the earth,
Its surface a mirror for the dead,
Its depths are a throat that swallows the living.
In 1925, the rains came,
And the waters rose like a beast unchained,
Dragging screams into the silt,
Burying them where the current hums.
A child's hand reached for the sky,
But the river does not forgive.
It keeps what it takes,
And it sings what it keeps—
A lullaby of bones,
A hymn of grief.

And so it begins…

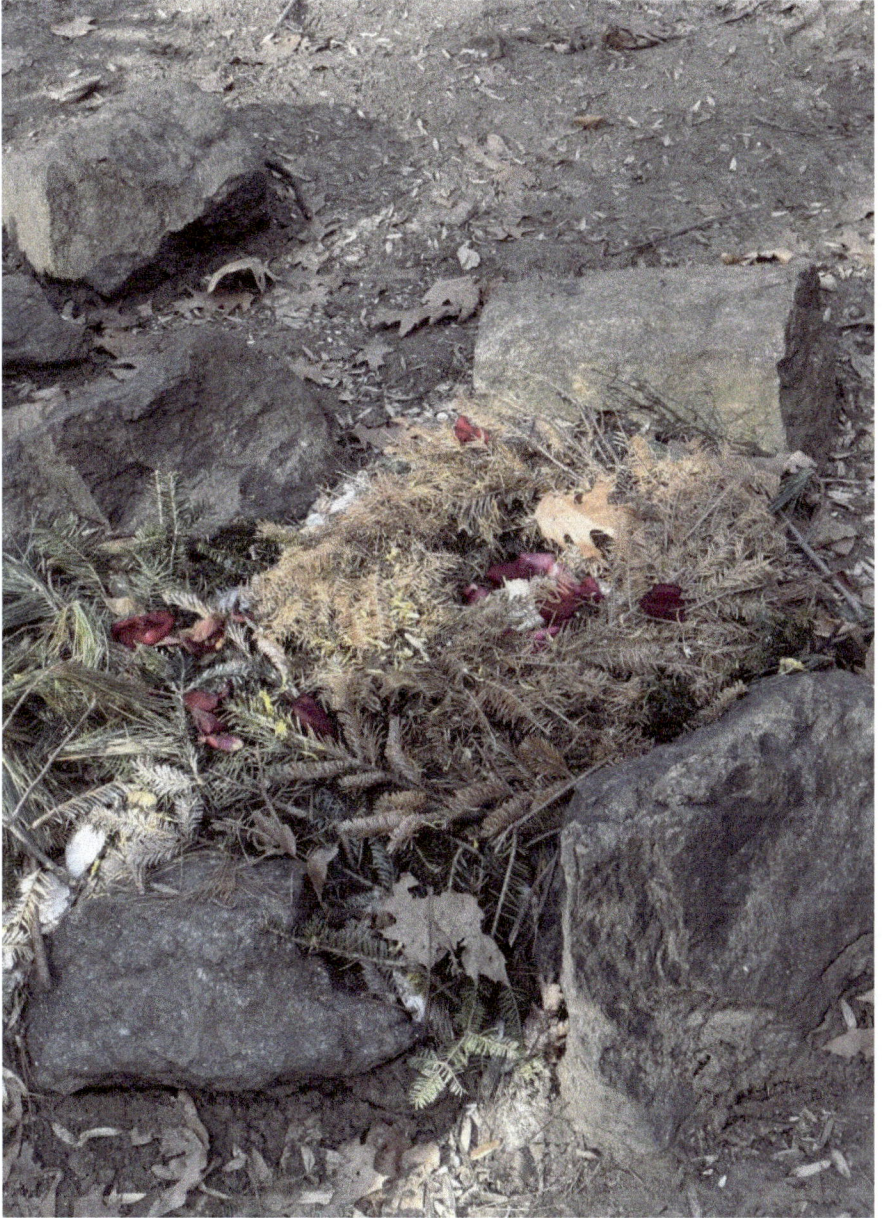

Anyone who stood on the cracked, wooden bridge could feel the thick air with the smell of decay and wet earth. It clung to you like soot, like a stain everyone carried around with them but never spoke of. Blackwater Hollow had not changed much in a decade. The same sagging houses miraculously withstood the test of times gone by. And the hollowed-eyed stares from the townspeople pierced through everything and everyone around them. The river still curled through the heart of the town like a serpent meant for vengeance. The water, the color of oil, sluggish and heavy reflecting the gray sky in fractured shards. Its surface rippled, as if something beneath was struggling to break free. It called out like a whisper at first and then a scream, a roar, that growled from the water, low and liquid. There were many times throughout the years when the river chose a victim. But Jimmy Charles, well, he was special. He had the gift. And the river didn't like that. It had its own religion and spirituality. There was no room for anyone else to share those blessings.

One late afternoon Jimmy Charles and his friends waded into the river for a swim. It was something they had done many times before. They were splashing around in the water, having a great time until laughter turned to screams as the current yanked Jimmy Charles under. He had been too slow, too scared and the river claimed him. The night he died many said they saw an unusual number of fireflies on the surface of the water and around its banks. Many heard whispers and they thought for sure they saw Jimmy Charles standing in the shallows. His skin, pale and his eyes as black as the water. Many left food offerings and other spiritual trinkets to ward off any evil. The visions of Jimmy Charles always faded but the river's pull didn't. It wanted more. It always had. It wanted me and I was just a babe at the time. Even at 10 years old I could still hear the hammering heart of the water calling for me. Back at the house, at mama's old cabin at the edge of the town I could feel its pull. The floorboards creaked under my boots and the air smelled of mildew and grief and I wondered what it was like before the water got hungry.

Mama said the river was never to be trusted but respected. And that it flowed through everyone's veins cold and endless. In its depths were faces, dozens of them. Mouths open in silent screams. Hands reaching up toward the surface. Mama said many of the townspeople saw muddy footprints in their homes, from feet wet and dirty. I knew mama was t telling the truth. And I never got too close to it. The river had my respect and my distance. I didn't see Jimmy Charles like many of the townspeople did. But I did see the Whisperwraiths. Their spectral, humanoid features always haunted the Appalachian Mountains. Gaunt, elongated, translucent, with ashy gray skin that glowed in the moonlight; their faces, featureless except for hollow, glowing eyes, and their limbs ended in claw-like tendrils that stretched and twisted unnaturally. They don't speak but emit a low, harmonic hum that sounds like whispered chants, luring victims into the forest. That's another place that had my respect. The forest. Everything here is surrounded by ancient, mist-shrouded peaks, and the locals have all withheld secrets about the hums that echo the mountains at night, and the river that follows you until you don't come back. This isn't just Appalachian folklore. It lives in our souls, it's who we are.

In the heart of the Appalachian gloom,
Where shadows twist beneath a shrouded moon,
A river runs, its waters black and deep,
The Whisperwraiths, their cursed vigil keep.
Its currents coil through ancient, gnarled stone,
A serpent's path, where lost winds moan.
No fish dart here, no heron dares to wade,
For death's cold breath haunts this cursed glade.
The Whisperwraiths, those spectral, tattered souls,
Drift over the waves where starlight never falls.
Their voices weave a soft, unholy hymn,
A dirge that chills the heart and clouds the mind.
"Stay back," they hum, their words like winter's bite,
Yet pull you close with promises of night.
They speak of secrets buried in the flow,
Of lives they claimed in ages long ago.
The river's edge is lined with bones and moss,
A graveyard born of those who dared to cross.
Its waters whisper, "Step, and you are mine,"
And Wraiths entwine your soul with spectral vine.
No map charts this, no trail leads to its shore,
Yet wanderers find it, drawn by phantom lore.
The river knows your name, your fears, your pain,
And Whisperwraiths will sing you to their chain.
So heed the tales the mountain folk retell,
Of waters dark where cursed spirits dwell.
For in that stream, where shadows writhe and roam,
The Whisperwraiths will claim you as their own.

RESOUND

Beneath the moon's unyielding glare,

The river Resound carves despair.

Its waters black, with secrets deep,

It hoards the souls it claims to keep.

Through jagged cliffs and shadowed vale,

It winds, a cold, unyielding trail.

Miners, bold with pick and flame,

Descend to seek their fleeting fame.

But Resound hungers, swift and sly,

Its currents drag their dreams to die.

Beneath the waves, their echoes fade,

Their bones entwine with silted shade.

Whisperwraiths, with hollow cries,

Haunt the banks where starlight dies.

Their voices weave through mist and pine,

A chilling song, a fatal sign.

Hikers tread with hearts alight,

Unwary of the creeping night.

The wraiths, with whispers soft as death,

Steal the air from mortal breath.

Townsfolk vanish, one by one,

Their names are forgotten by the sun.

And children, drawn by fleeting gleams,

Chase fireflies through haunted dreams.

The river calls with silvered lies,

Reflecting stars in mirrored skies.

Small hands reach out, too young to know,

The Resound's pull will not let go.

The wraiths, they laugh, a spectral din,

As innocence is drawn within.

No cross, no prayer can break its thrall,

No light can pierce its darkened call.

The river Resound, with wraiths entwined,

Claims the body, soul, and mind.

Its waters churn, its whispers sing,

A requiem for everything.

I can't tell you how it came to pass but somehow I became the guardian of the mountains with its peaks jagged against the twilight sky. Some say, the land chose me to be its folklorist although I never went around chasing stories. Things happened and they became part of me, part of the mountains and its people. Many don't believe in monsters but they are real. They live among the rustle of leaves and in the deep waters and in the choirs of unpleasant singing that drifts through open windows at night, and in the oppressive air that strangles you while you sleep. Tales of hikers gone missing and miners vanishing without a trace in the 1880s still haunt the place, sending shivers down everyone's spine. And then there's the glowing stone buried deep in the mountains that appears and disappears at will as if possessed by some otherworldly entity. I've heard the mountain and the river whisper my name. Charlotta Dee-come see…but I don't listen. The words may slither through the room and beyond it, from the forest beyond the cabin but I rebuke them. I always look out my window at night and see the shadows in the moonlight and the faint glow of flickering lights between the trees, but I stay put even though it tugs at me like a swift current, hypnotic and cruel.

One night I heard the hum and it stuck in my head like a lament and lullaby that beckoned to be explored. Before I knew it, I was walking, my boots crunching on the forest floor. I was led to a narrow ravine, and the air grew colder. I stumbled over the root of a tree and caught myself on a rock. It beamed and glittered in the earth. It was quartz streaked with veins of black, and it was pulsating faintly with an inner light. It was then that I saw them. Three figures emerged from the darkness. They were tall, thin, their skin translucent, shimmering like frost. Their eyes glowed a sickly green and their tentacle-like claws stretched out toward me quivering with anticipation. There was a chant of sorrow and hunger emanating from them. Join us, feel us, free us, fear us. I tried to scream but couldn't. I froze in terror. One of them lunged at me. Its tendrils wrapped around my wrist. My skin burned but I yanked my hand back and managed to break free. I ran as fast as I could as it chased me. I didn't stop until I reached the cabin, slamming the door behind me, collapsing against it, my heart pounding so hard I felt faint. There were dozens of voices on the other side of the door pleading for help, my help. "I can't help you!" I screamed, holding my hands to my ears, trying to drown out the horrible calls for help. And then a single voice, cold and clear, "You'll come back. Souls like you always do."

Through moonlit woods, she weaves her flight,

A woman touched by sacred light.

Her spirit hums with ancient grace,

A psychic glow upon her face.

Three entities, with eyes of coal,

Pursue her path, their whispers cold.

A dozen lost souls trail behind,

Their hollow cries entwine her mind.

"Help us," they plead, their voices thin,

Bound by grief, by guilt, by sin.

Her heart, a beacon, feels their pain,

Yet fear drives her through shadowed rain.

The trees bend low, their branches claw,

As spectral winds howl what they saw.

The entities, with knowing sneers,

Chase her steps through primal fears.

Her home appears, a fragile keep,

Where sacred runes her secrets steep.

She slips inside, bolts lock, heart pounds,

Yet echoes linger—haunting sounds.

"You'll return," the entities hiss,

Their voices snake through midnight's kiss.

"Souls like yours, they always do,

To mend the loss, to guide them through."

She breathes, her spirit fierce, unbroken,

Her mystic call remains unspoken.

For though she fled, her truth holds fast—

The woods will call her back at last.

LOW MURMURS

Mama was mad I didn't heed her warnings. She grabbed me by the arms and reprimanded me before giving me a big hug of relief and holding me in her arms. She said I was lucky to be alive and that it was probably because I had many gifts, many blessings, that the forest wanted to see developed. They were always watching. The eyes of the forest. I could feel their stare even when I was a babe in mama's arms. I slept with mama that night, in the sanctuary of her room, where herbs and potions, candles and whispered spells loomed. But the woods were never silent, and so mama hummed lullabies until I slept into dreams. And in my dreams I felt the forest's pulse and the river's motion, and mama's voice humming and saying, "Pay them no mind."

The seasons passed and one frostbitten night when I was sixteen I saw him, Jimmy Charles. He didn't look like a ghost or anything like that, he was solid, like me, like mama. He stared at me from the foot of my bed as a bunch of covers kept me warm. He didn't talk but he pointed to the wood burning fireplace. There was a protective shift in the room, as if he was doing it. But I also knew it was a warning. He was trying to tell me something, I could see it in his eyes. They were glinting with knowing. I knew what he was trying to say. "Stay inside." As I stared at him, my soul let him know that I got his message, and then he disappeared. I saw him from the window as he stepped into the dark. His silhouette, swallowed by the trees.

Hours passed before the murmurs came and swelled against the cabin walls. Mama hurriedly came into my room and put an amethyst necklace around my neck, one that she had spiritually fixed. She wore one just like mine, protection from above, from the ancestors. Mama's heart was pounding so fast I swear I could hear it as she clutched the amethyst necklace in her hands and pleaded to the spirits; her face frozen in terror and her eyes wide, and unseeing. When the murmurs stopped the silence came, and that was much worse. It was heavy and it lingered, choking the air. Hours passed and all seemed well until Mama got sick.

She clutched her chest and said, "Get some salt and iron. It will help banish the spirits. Wear your protective charm. Never take it off." And with that, she died. The mountains had claimed my mama just like it did my poppa before I was born. At least that's what mama said. I buried her in a cove by our property under a yew tree. That's where she said she wanted to be when she entered the spirit realm. I did as she asked. I always obeyed her but the loneliness and grief have dulled my magic. And I have never ever felt this way before. I could always rely on magic for everything. For healing, for protection, for cooking, for hexing and yes, sometimes I did my share of that. I considered it a form of self care when the townspeople branded mama and me as witches and ostracized us like we were nothing. The spirits always did my bidding and the townspeople started to realize that. So much so that it scared them. And even though they pointed at me with stares and gossip, they managed to leave me alone out of fear. And that was all I wanted. I never fit in, never had any real friends, and I was fine with that. I had mama. She was all that for me and more. My best friend, my mama, my protector, my teacher, and now she is gone. Grief has dulled my magic and the spirits I once communed with have grown distant as if they themselves are afraid.

Beneath the yew, where shadows creep,

Mama lies in endless sleep.

Her grave, a cradle carved in loam,

The witch's heart, her mother's home.

The roots entwine her silent frame,

Whisper secrets, speak her name.

No stone to mark, no hymn to sing,

Just wind's soft moan, a mourner's wing.

Her daughter kneels, her hands in dirt,

Each clod a wound, each tear a hurt.

The yew stands guard, its boughs like shrouds,

Its berries, red as grief's dark clouds.

Once she wove the moon's pale light,

Chased the spirits through the night.

Now her voice is earth's low hum,

A pulse where wilder magic drums.

The stars above, they dimly gleam,

Through branches bent by time's old dream.

Mama's soul, the roots now keep,

Beneath the yew, in endless sleep.

FLOOD AND FOWL

Years passed. I'm in my 20s now and I've honed my craft. My psychic senses are razor- sharp, and the murmurs still haunt me. They return at twilight, slithering through the pines, whispering my name. The townspeople know they speak to me, the dead. Some have sought me out for messages from their deceased loved ones. They pay me and I'm grateful for it, even as they fear me and keep their distance in public. It's a strange position to be in; a confidant in private and a marginalized person in public. I know all their secrets, and yet they act like they've never seen me before in their life. It may be different if I attended their church services, and held the Bible in my hands as a sign of faith, but my faith isn't up for display and it's internal. The best way I can describe it is like when I hear the ancestors speaking in fragments from another dimension, curses in forgotten tongues, cries of betrayal. They're not really spirits, the ancestors. They're older, hungrier, bound to the land's blood soaked history. Massacres, rituals, broken pacts, the mountains remember. You can't fight them. They're inside of you and they're the land's wrath. I tried once. To fight them. I wanted to be normal like the others, to not see things before they happened and to drown out the voices of the dead. But they took me. I passed out and convulsed and each one of them started to pass through me. I was the vessel. And as my knees buckled, they infused me with their power, their blood and made me keep their vigil. It's the witch's cycle, my mama used to say. A witch's life can be snuffed out, she could flee, or at least try to, but they would always find another. Mama said some witches ended it, by their own trembling hands. But they never rested in peace after that. I learned to give in. To keep my promise to stay on the mountain and never leave it. To accept the isolation and the company as it came and went. I solidified the pact when I drew a sigil into the earth, carved it in there good, a binding spell with the land itself, forbidden and final. Blood dripped from my palm sealing the pact, fierce and unbroken. I poured my magic, my life into the spell, tethering the voices to my soul, and silence fell true and deep. The Appalachians sighed their secrets safe with me.

In the heart of the Appalachians, where shadows weave and cling,
The mountains hum with ancient songs no mortal throat could sing.
Beneath the mist, a witch abides, her eyes like embers glow,
Commanding flood and fowl as one, where wild, dark rivers flow.
The ridges rise, their granite bones etched sharp against the sky,
Yet bow to her, the crone of storms, whose voice makes tempests cry.
She lifts her hands, and rivers roar, unleashed from earthen veins,
The flood obeys, a serpent swift, devouring fields and lanes.
The holler drowns, the waters surge, a tide of churning wrath,
Swallowing trails and hemlock groves that dare to cross its path.
Her laughter cracks like thunderheads, as streams her will abide,
Carving scars through ancient hills where secrets long reside.
And fowl, they heed her whispered call, from sparrow to the crow,
Their wings are a storm of feathered blades that darken as they go.
From sycamore to red oak's crown, they swarm at her decree,
A legion fierce, with talons sharp, to guard her sovereignty.
The witch of Appalachia stands, where flood and fowl entwine,
Her power was born of root and rain, of claw and crooked pine.
The mountains kneel, the heavens quake, her magic holds them fast,
A queen of chaos, crowned in a storm, whose reign shall ever last.

DISSOLUTION

In the heart of Appalachia, where mists curl tight,
Lives a witch, cloaked in shadow, born of the night.
Her roots sink deep in the mountain's old bones,
Bound to its whispers, its secrets, its stones.
She was young when the magic first sparked in her veins,
A fire unbidden, both blessing and chain.
The hills sang her name, their voices a vow:
 "You are ours, forever—surrendered, now."
Her power unfurls like a storm's jagged breath,
Commanding the roots, bending life, weaving death.
She speaks to the rivers, they answer her call,
The trees bow in reverence, their branches her thrall.
Yet dissolution creeps, soft as a sigh,
In the frost-bitten dawns, in the owl's mournful cry.
Her magic's a tether, eternal, unyielding,
A cage of her making, its edges unpeeling.
She cannot depart, though her heart may still roam,
The mountains, her cradle, her prison, her home.
Each spell that she casts binds her deeper within,
Her soul woven tight to the earth's ancient skin.
No lover may linger, no child bear her name,
For the hills claim her whole, both her glory and shame.
Yet she stands, unbowed, with a crown of wild flame,
Her power accepted, her spirit the same.
The wind hums her legend, through valleys it weaves,
Of a witch who is mighty, yet never can leave.
In the heart of the mountains, where shadows abide,
She reigns, fierce and boundless, with nowhere to hide.

In the shadowed folds of the Appalachian mountains, where mist clung to the pines like a lover's whisper, I felt my father's presence for the first time. It wasn't a feeling like I had with the others, the dead, this was different. The sky and the trees were knotted with secrets and spells, tucked deep in the woods where the sun barely reached. I'm known by almost everyone, including all those in neighboring towns, for my craft. They all come to me when they need herbs that heal fevers, charms that turn away evil fortune, and love spells that bend the will of the receiver. I am that voice that could coax truth from the wind. That's what they said about me, half in awe, half in fear. They spoke about me often and mama too, but they never mentioned my father. Mama swore he was taken by a fever before my first cry split the night. But I knew she wasn't exactly telling me the truth, although I never questioned her on it. I kept my knowledge quiet, letting it sit deep within me. Everything reveals itself at the right time, and I just figured the right time hadn't come yet. I didn't need anyone but mama anyway. She taught me the old ways, how to read the stars, how to bind a wound with spider silk, and how to listen to the crows when they spoke of danger. Mama's magic was quieter, worn by years of grief. Mine was louder, more challenging, born of retribution and pain.

When I got a bit older I used to ask mama about my father. I wanted to know what he was like. She'd say, "He was a good man, but he's gone. Let it rest." Being a respectful daughter, young and trusting, I didn't pester much on the subject. I saw her eyes cloud up when I mentioned him and I felt it was best to leave well enough alone. His absence gnawed at me like a splinter under skin. But I kept my mouth shut. I imagined him as being a tall figure with kind eyes, lost to time, His bones resting somewhere beneath the mountain roots. And I took comfort in that, even though I knew in my heart and soul he wasn't. I felt him alive. Very much alive. And I knew one day I would find out the truth. The truth reveals itself in fragments. It's a contrast to deception. A reflection of how we learn.A philosophical view of being. And the dangers of incomplete information.

BREED

In the heart of Appalachia, where shadows weave through ancient
    pines,
A witch treads softly, her soul entwined with signs.
Her blood hums with secrets, old as the mountains' weathered stone,
She speaks to the dead, whispering to her own.
By a creek's low murmur, beneath a moon that bleeds pale light,
A specter forms, her father's face, long lost to endless night.
"Not dead," he breathes through mist and time, his voice a jagged
    thread,
"I live, my child, where ancients breed, where truths are born and
    bled."
The Anunnaki, star-born kin, their eyes like molten flame,
In caverns deep, where cryptids creep, they call her by her name.
Mothman's wings stir midnight air, his omens carved in frost,
Bigfoot's tread shakes earth's old bones, their lineage intercrossed.
Her power pulses, a vein of magic raw and wild,
Her father's blood, a witch's flood, the mountains' sacred child.
The dead relay their secrets, of breeding rites in shadowed glades,
Where Anunnaki seed the earth, and cryptids guard the shades.
She walks the ridge, her heart a forge, her spirit fierce and free,
A conduit for voices lost, for powers yet to be.
In Appalachian hollows, where breed and blood align,
She reigns, the witch of ghosts, her father's truth divine.

I saw my father in my dreams. He was in a cave-riddled ridge not ten miles from my cabin. The townspeople said he had been a preacher once. A famous one around these parts. Not the fire and brimstone kind but a man who saw God in nature. In the rustle of trees and the pulse of the earth. His faith was wild, untamed and many took exception to that. It clashed with the rigid doctrine of the other preachers whose sermons dripped with judgment. Legend has it that Rev. Hall and my father, Amos clashed over a ritual he performed. A cleansing of a cursed river that had claimed many lives. They said my dad used chants older than the church's cornerstone. Hall called it devilry and accused my father of witchcraft as the town rallied against him. The night I was born, they came. A mob with torches blazing, intent on making my father pay for the evil they claimed he had done. In order to protect mama and me, he took off into the mountains at night, leaving behind a lie that he had perished with fever, when in fact, many believed he had perished in the wild. Nonetheless, he was never seen or heard of again, and no one ever really talked about him at great length either. Mama included. Mama was heartbroken but fierce and she sought to keep the truth hidden even if she had to threaten everyone with magic. And it worked. The truth stayed buried and my father was dead to shield me from shame, danger and exile. I'm in my late 20s now and I feel the weight of that lie. I see visions of my father, still alive, bearded, weathered with eyes like my own. After that night, the town folk grew sick. Rev. Hall died like many others, crops wilted and wells soured. There were whispers about a witch in the woods and her daughter who sought revenge. And other preachers spoke of that kind of thing, branding us both for life. It was worse than putting a noose around our necks, that would have been more merciful. Mama's silence grew heavier with each passing day. A wall I could not breach.

IDOLATRY

When Millicent Hoffman came to see me for a reading and some healing herbs, she mentioned my father. I kept my mouth shut and let her talk, giving her the side eye every now and then. Milllicent Hoffman loved to talk. She was like the town's Daily Gazette. A busy body who pretended to be everyone's friend but backstabbed them any chance she got. The woman had no salvation in her soul and poison ruled her tongue. I don't know if the story she told me about my father was true or not, but I listened without giving her any reaction at all. It upset her some but she just went on talking and talking. She talked so much that day that I got dizzy. I mean physically ill, dizzy. When she finally switched subjects, I asked her to come back another day and told her money quickly while escorting her out the door.

She said my father, Amos, preached in a clapboard church, and his congregation of weathered folk with calloused hands hung on his every word as he held a carved wooden cross, its edges worn smooth by years of fervent sermons. She said my father used to call it, his anchor to the divine, swearing it channeled God's wrath against sin. The cross was no mere symbol, it was his idol, a talisman he believed held the power to smite all evil. He raised it high, eyes blazing, promising salvation to those who knelt before it.

Townspeople spoke of my mother too. They said she was a witch, who could hex a man's crops or charm a storm to stillness. Funny how they all talked but came to us when they needed some good health spells or retribution. The one thing mama refused to ever do was love spells. She said it just wasn't right to tie someone's will like that. That love should always be freely given and freely received. It was the one thing this world had that was pure and not tainted. Ms. Millicent went on to describe my mother's altar. She said other people were talking about it, but in fact, it was her. She was my mama's client for a long time.

She said that the altar held a gnarled root shaped like a woman's silhouette, draped in feathers and bones. And Ms. Millicent would be right about that. It was an ancestor, a spirit-kin, and its ancient magic was tethered to us and to the mountains. We kept it for protection, and guidance. Mama often lit candles around it, muttering incantations that she taught me to do. It gave us domination over life's unseen currents. The idol was power incarnate and we paid reverence to it as such.

In our house faith lingered free. That's how I saw it anyway, by the stories that were told to me about my father and the experiences I had with my mama. Here in the Appalachian mountains, everyone clings to their idols, but they also realize that the real power wasn't in wood or bone or feathers, but in the hands that worked to either heal or hurt.

The Idol's Truth

In a town where shadows clung to stone,
A gilded idol stood alone.
Its eyes of jade, its crown of gold,
Held hearts in thrall, both young and old.
The preacher railed with fervent cries,
"Cast down this god, its power lies!"
He swung his cross, his voice a flame,
Condemning worship, cursing shame.
The witch, with herbs and whispered lore,
Knelt by the idols, seeking more.
Her fingers traced their weathered face,
Murmuring spells for truth's embrace.
The townsfolk gathered, torn in two,
Some prayed, some cursed, their fears grew.
They clutched their charms, their crosses, stones,
Believing power lived in bones.
The idols gleamed beneath the moon,
Silent, still, they offered nothing soon.
Yet in their glow, the truth took flight—
No sparks divine, no sacred might.
The preacher paused, his cross held low,
The witch's eyes began to glow.
"The power's not in gold or clay,"
She whispered softly, "but in our way."
The townsfolk stirred, their murmurs ceased,
The preacher's heart, at last, released.

"No idol heals, no idol harms—
The strength lies here, in human arms."
Together then, they turned their gaze,
From lifeless stone to living days.
For hurt or healing, love or pain,
The power's theirs—to wield, refrain.
The idol stood, but none would bow,
Its reign had ended, broken now.
In witch's spell, in preacher's word,
The townsfolk's truth at last was heard.

PRIMAL BLOOD

The rivers spoke of it all. Primal blood. There are songs about balance being broken, and of faith turned to obsession. There's a new river now, older and deeper, hummed with cycles, of idols rising and falling, of powers summoned and forgotten. They carried the story downstream, where fishers and washerwomen heard it in the water's cadence: a warning that idolatry, however devout, could wake things best left sleeping.

The beings faded, in and out, slipping back through the veil, though some swore they still saw eyes in the river's depths and in the hollow of tall trees. Their idols had shaped their lives—given them hope, bound them to fear, and opened doors to the unknown. The mountains stood silent, watched without a reveal, but the rivers never stopped talking, whispering of the thin line between faith and folly, and the shadows that waited just beyond.

Otherworldly beings neither angels nor demons, but something older, born of the mountain's marrow, kept vigil.

They were shadows with many limbs, voices like the wind through broken glass, drawn by the faith poured into wood and roots. A primal blood that poured red. An instinctual nature, born of heritage and kinship. A life force and vitality that fed the Appalachians with resilience and foundation.

These beings didn't bring healing or destruction—they watched, they whispered, they waited.

To the townspeople, they were a terror and a wonder. A reminder that their idols held power they barely understood.

And the beings, well, they lingered, slipping through dreams, brushing through the edges of the forest and beyond. Their presence, a weight on every heart.

In the heart of Appalachia, where the mountains claw the sky,
Primal blood runs thick as coal, where ancient spirits lie.
The ridges hum with secrets old, their whispers carved in stone,
Otherworldly beings walk the mist, their presence never shown.
The holler's breath is heavy, steeped in heritage and kin,
Ancestors' bones beneath the earth, their voices sing within.
A witch, she dwells in shadow's edge, with roots that twist and bind,
Her spells are woven from the stars, her heart the mountain's mind.
The preacher stands on hallowed ground, his bible worn and thin,
He calls to God, but trembling knows the spirits' ceaseless din.
His sermons clash with primal roars, where faith and fear collide,
For in these hills, the old ones reign, and none can ever hide.
The river runs, a haunted vein, through valleys deep and wide,
Its waters sing of blood and bone, of souls that never died.
It carries cries of long-lost clans, their anguish cold as stone,
And mirrors shapes that shift and fade, not human, yet not gone.
The people here, of rugged stock, their blood a primal flame,
Are tied to earth, to root, to rock, to powers without name.
The witch's chant, the preacher's prayer, the river's endless wail,
All blend beneath the mountain's gaze, where otherworlds prevail.
In Appalachia's shadowed heart, where heritage holds sway,
The living and the lost converge, in night's eternal play.
Primal blood and spectral kin forever guard the land,
Bound to mountains, rivers, souls, by an unseen, ancient hand.

MARRIAGE

Marriage was something I never even thought of until well into my early thirties when I met him. He was no stranger to whispers and gossip himself. Being the preacher's son at the time held him up to a higher standard than most and the townspeople watched him carefully with a critical eye. His name was Jonah. He was all sharp angles and soft eyes with a voice that could sooth a storm. Many had already chastised him for not marrying young but he didn't seem to care about that. He was also in his early thirties, and the discerning kind, deep, with emotional maturity that could handle all the snide comments thrown his way. He carried his father's Bible but without all the fire and brimstone Rev. Weatherly had in his heart. Our eyes first met when he was helping Clara load her horse and buggy with items from the general store. He was the first to ever look me in the eye, to make that contact. He tipped his hat and smiled. And the air crackled, not with magic but with something older, hungrier. I couldn't tell if it was a blessing or a bad omen then. I guess I was too emotionally involved just by that first encounter to see clearly, to read the signs. "Beautiful day," he said. And I smiled back at him, while Clara gave me the side eye and a scoff. I lingered close by until Clara left. She gave me one more scoff as she took off, just to let me know how much she didn't approve of my presence. Jonah came over to speak to me. He was so polite and kind, genuine or so it seemed. We spoke of small things at first: the way frost painted the ferns, the songs of the river and the nearby leaves on a tree when the wind hit them just right. Soon, he was stopping by the cabin just to check on me and to say, "hello." Words turned to touches and touches to a love that burned recklessly. We married one another in our hearts with our souls, but Jonah was bound by his father's God and the expectations of the townspeople. He knew we were forbidden. I didn't care. I didn't answer to anyone but the mountain. But he was different. We met in secret. In moonlit clearings and hidden caves, our love, a quiet rebellion against everyone and everything that opposed it. We married one another in a ceremony older than any church, in the open air where the mountains and all its inhabitants watched without making a single sound. We wove rings of willow and put it on one another's fingers, and took vows under a canopy of stars. Our witnesses, the owls and ancient oaks. For a while we were whole. We lived in my cabin where he wrote and read poetry to me by candlelight. But the mountains like the townspeople were unkind to things that didn't fit. Jonah's father preached from the pulpit about sin and sorcery, his eyes boring into his son. Jonah began to falter. And that was the beginning of the end for us.

Jonah was torn between me and the world he had always known. And then came Clara, the miller's daughter with her perfect smile, smooth white skin and Sunday dresses. Her laughter, free of shadows and secrets. She was everything the townspeople wanted for Jonah, pious, proper, safe. He resisted at first. I saw it in him before he ever did. My soul knew but I loved him from the moment we first laid eyes on one another and I dismissed what I should have listened to. That interior voice that tells you he's going to break your heart. Yet, you trust, and you give in. You hope, and you persevere. And after all that, you break. And you break hard. Knowing your first instinct was correct and you should have listened. I could have done a love spell to get him back. But mama had always taught me that you can't tie someone's will when it comes to love. That it should always be freely given and freely received because it was the one pure thing in this world that we had and that we took with us when we died. So I let him go. Magic could bind the wind but not a heart. One night as fireflies danced over the river, I unbound the willow ring from his finger. "Go," I said. "You were never mine to keep." Jonah wept but he left. His footsteps, fading in the dark.

He married Clara in the church in front of the townspeople and in front of his father's approving gaze. And it was as if everything and everyone sighed in relief. As if order had been restored.

I never held any grudges. Instead I sought out to help the other women who came to me in the dead of night, seeking courage to defy their own cages. And I gained their respect. And I dare say, their love.

When I was in my fifties I saw him one last time. He passed by my cabin, with graying hair. He stood and paused for a mere second, and there was a flicker of regret in his chest. I held my ground and just smiled. The wind carried my scent of sage and sorrow. And he walked on. Back to a life that fit him, and a world that never would.

Beneath the ancient peaks where shadows creep,
In Appalachia's heart, where secrets sleep,
Lived a witch with starlit eyes,
Her magic spun in whispers, soft as sighs.
The preacher's son, bold and fair,
With sunlight in his smile, he met her there.
By moon-glowed streams, their hearts began to race,
A love forbidden, in that sacred place.
No chapel bound their vows, no bells did ring,
They wed in wilds, where nightshade blooms sing.
Her spells wove round his heart, his touch her flame,
In hidden hollows, none could know their name.
The town, all righteous, scorned their tangled bond,
His father's wrath, a fire to respond.
"You'll wed a girl of virtue, pure and tame!"
He chose Clara, blessed by the church's name.
Jonah faltered, torn by love and fear,
The town's approval called, its voice so clear.
He left Charlotta Dee, with a final plea,
"My heart is yours, but I can't live free."
She stood alone where hemlocks softly sway,
Her grief a storm no magic could allay.
He married Clara, in a church of stone,
The townsfolk cheered, their will now his own.
Charlotta Dee haunts the ridges, wild and lone,
She chants a dirge, her heart a heavy stone.
Jonah lives, a life of proper guise,
with dreams of her beneath the mountain skies.

THE DARKSOME STATESMAN

In shadows deep, where whispers creep and coil,
A statesman treads, his heart a barren soil.
His eyes, like embers, gleam with cold intent,
Each word a blade, each smile a dark portent.
Beneath the cloak of power, secrets seethe,
A labyrinth of lies his lips bequeath.
The chamber echoes with his silken voice,
Yet every vow obscures the people's choice.
His hands, though soft, wield chains none dare to see,
He carves his name in the shadows' sovereignty.
No light can pierce the mask he wears so well,
A prince of dusk, where darker counsels dwell.
The halls of state, once bright with hope's refrain,
Now bow beneath his calculated reign.
And though he speaks of justice, grand and free,
His heart beats cold—a darksome mystery.

A new figure we all called The Dark Statesman cast a long, dark shadow over the town. He just appeared as a resident one day, and his presence caused immediate fear. His demeanor was rough, jagged just like the outline of the mountain. He fit in with the natural ruggedness, with its asperity, coarseness and rawness. It was as if the mountains themselves had birthed him. He had grit and harshness and commanded respect but gave none out. He was a man of sharp suits and sharper ambition. His name was Gideon Kelly, a politician exiled from the glittering capitals, for scandals too numerous to name, now slinking into town like a snake in the grass, to rebuild his empire in the isolation of the mountains.

His manor, a looming edifice of black stone, squatted atop a ridge overlooking the town like a vulture eyeing carrion.

Gideon was a man of ruthless cunning, his smile as cold as the iron like the mines he'd swindled from the townsfolk. He'd promised jobs, prosperity, and progress, but delivered only misery. Taxes soared, homes were seized, and the local council bent to his will, their pockets lined with his bribes. He strode through town with a sneer, his polished boots clicking on the cobblestones, while the people whispered curses behind closed doors. His cruelty was subtle but sharp—widows lost their pensions, children went hungry, and dissenters found their crops mysteriously burned.

The Darksome Statesman ruled not with a scepter, but with fear.
Yet, for all his power, Gideon's heart—or what passed for one—was snared by a woman who cared nothing for his influence. Charlotta Dee was that woman, the witch. She was no storybook crone; her eyes like storm clouds and hair that caught the moonlight like raven feathers attracted him. Even in her late 50s she was beautiful and looked much younger for her age. Her magic was old, drawn from the roots of the mountains, and she brewed remedies for the sick, wove charms for the desperate, and spoke to the spirits that lingered in the pines after all these years. The townsfolk revered her, though they feared her too, for her power was wild and unbound. Nothing much had changed in that respect.

Gideon first saw her at the harvest market, her stall draped in herbs and bones, her gaze cutting through him like a blade. He approached, all charm and swagger, offering her a place at his side, a share in his wealth, a chance to "rise above this mud-soaked town." Charlotta Dee's laughter was a whipcrack, sharp and unyielding. "I'd sooner bed a rattlesnake," she said, her voice low and dangerous. "Your coin's no good here, and neither is your heart." The crowd hushed, and Gideon's face darkened, but he retreated, his pride stung.

He did not relent. Gifts arrived at Charlotta Dee's cabin—silks, jewels, deeds to land stolen from the poor. She burned them all, the smoke curling into sigils that warded her home from his influence. He sent letters, promising power, protection, even love, but Charlotta Dee's replies were crows that dropped the torn parchment at his doorstep. His obsession grew, a festering wound. He began to sabotage her work, spreading lies that her remedies were poison, her charms were curses. When that failed, he sent his lackeys to harass her, but the forest itself seemed to protect her—men returned limping, swearing the trees had moved, the shadows had bitten.

Gideon's cruelty worsened as his frustration mounted. He doubled taxes, shuttered the school, and let the mines collapse, blaming the workers for his own greed. The townsfolk, ground down, began to whisper of rebellion, but fear of Gideon's wrath kept them silent. Charlotta Dee, however, was not so easily cowed. One moonless night, she slipped into town, her cloak blending with the dark. She painted sigils on the manor's gates, old symbols that hummed with power, and whispered a spell that carried on the wind: "What you sow, you shall reap."

The next morning, Gideon woke to find his manor choked with thorns, their barbs dripping with a black sap that burned the skin. His mirrors showed not his face, but hers, laughing. His voice faltered in council, his lies unraveling as if spoken by a child. The townsfolk, emboldened, began to resist. Petitions turned to protests, protests to torches. Gideon, desperate, stormed Charlotta Dee's cabin, only to find it empty, the hearth cold. She was gone, but her magic lingered. His crops withered, his gold turned to ash, and the spirits of the mountains whispered his sins to all who passed.

By winter, Gideon was a shadow of himself, his manor crumbling, his power broken. The townsfolk, led by Charlotta Dee's quiet allies, drove him from town, his name a curse on their lips. Charlotta Dee returned to the cabin to the town, her laughter echoing in the wind. Some say she became the wind itself, guarding the mountains from men like the Darksome Statesman. But all agreed: in this town, in the Appalachian mountains, the witch's will was stronger than any man's greed.

CONDEMNING THOUGHTS

In the heart of the Appalachian hills,
Where the moon casts shadows and the night wind chills,
A witch dwells alone, her name cursed and scorned,
Her spirit, a tapestry, tattered and torn.
They whisper of her with condemning breath,
In hamlets below, where fear courts death.
"Her eyes hold the devil, her hands weave his art,"
They damn her with venom, they tear her apart.
In a cabin of secrets, where moss clings to stone,
She brews her old magic, her soul's undertone.
The townsfolk revile her, their voices a blade,
Yet she carries their hatred, unbowed, unafraid.
Far off in the wildwood, where shadows conspire,
A cave holds a man, once preacher, now sire.
Her father, long vanished, a conjurer bold,
Whose black magic whispered of powers untold.
He walked with the gospel, then turned to the dark,
His heart split by starlight, his faith but a spark.
Banished by shame, he fled to the wood,
Hiding from judgment, from all that once stood.
Years carved their story in wrinkles and stone,
His beard white as winter, his spirit alone.
Yet whispers of her, his daughter, his kin,
Stirred embers of longing, a pull from within.
One night, 'neath a moon like a sickle of frost,

He crept from his cave, seeking her, tempest-tossed.

The pines seemed to murmur, the ridges to sigh,

As he found her small cabin, where embers don't die.

She stood at her threshold, her gaze sharp as flint,

Her voice, like the wind through a cedar's coarse hint.

"Father," she said, with a heart cold as clay,

"Why come now, after years gone astray?"

His eyes, dim with sorrow, held secrets and pain,

"I'm bound for the shadow, won't see you again.

I preached of salvation, then conjured the night,

But I loved you, my daughter, though I fled from the light."

The townsfolk still cursed her, their hatred a flame,

But she saw in his face neither guilt nor true shame.

"You left me to carry the weight of their scorn,

A witch they named me, from the day I was born."

He reached out a hand, gnarled as roots of the oak,

And whispered of spells that the darkness once spoke.

"I taught myself the old ways, the craft in your bones,

But love was my failing, not magic's sharp tones."

She wavered, her heart caught in memory's snare,

Of a father who vanished, yet left her to bear

The chants and the curses, the fire and the dread,

While he hid in the shadows, where no light was shed.

"I'm dying," he rasped, "and I've come to atone,

To see you, my daughter, before I'm but bone."

Her eyes, fierce as starlight, softened with tears,

For the weight of their story, the loss of the years.

No words could unweave all the pain they had sown,

Yet she let him embrace her, their hearts not alone.

In the Appalachian night, where the wild spirits roam,

A witch and her father found peace for a home.

He left with the dawn, to his cave's final call,

A conjurer fading, where shadows still fall.

And she, though still damned by the tongues of the vale,

Kept their moment eternal, a bittersweet tale.

MIDNIGHT-FOG

In the cradle of the Appalachians, where secrets hum low,
The midnight fog weaves its shroud, a ghostly ebb and flow.
Beneath the ancient pines, where moonlight dares not creep,
A witch, born of starlight, stirs from a restless sleep.
Her father, a shadow, fled the night of her birth,
Cursed by his own blood, a heart heavy with worth.
To save her from the darkness that clawed at his soul,
He abandoned her to the mountains, where wild spirits roll.
Through years of whispered lore, she grew fierce and wise,
With spells in her veins and the moon in her eyes.
Yet the ache of his absence, a wound never healed,
Lingered like mist in the hollows, a truth unrevealed.
Tonight, the fog thickens, a veil soft and dire,
The air hums with secrets, alive with strange fire.
Creatures of the mountains—whispers, claws, and wings—
Rustle in the shadows, where the unseen sings.
He comes, a specter, through the mist's silver thread,
A man torn by time, by the choices that bled.
His eyes, like the fog, hold a sorrow profound,
"I left to protect you," he speaks, barely a sound.
"I'm cursed, my child, a beast in my core,
The mountains called me, to settle the score.
I fled to spare you the weight of my fate,
But now I must go, where no soul can wait."
The witch, her heart raging, a storm in her chest,
Reaches for the father she never knew best.
"Why now?" she cries, her voice sharp as a blade,
"Why show me your face, then let memory fade?"
He steps back, the fog curling tight round his frame,
"I came to say goodbye, to speak your true name."
The mountains growl softly, their secrets awake,
As the fog claims his form, like a tide's endless break.
A portal yawns open, a rift in the night,
Stars spin in its depths, a kaleidoscope's flight.
To another universe, where shadows may roam,

He steps through the veil, forever from home.
The creatures of the hollows, with eyes like old flame,
Watch silent as the fog swallows all but his name.
The witch stands alone, her heart fierce and torn,
Bound to the mountains where her spirit was born.
The midnight fog lingers, heavy with grief,
Carrying whispers of love, of loss, of belief.
In the Appalachian night, where secrets abide,
She weaves her own magic, with the stars as her guide.

WEIGHTS AND WOE

In the Appalachian hollows, where the shadows twist and moan,
A witch kneels in solitude, her heart a heavy stone.
Her father, newly dead, his breath stolen by the night,
Leaves her orphaned in the mist, adrift in fading light.
The mountains cradle her sorrow, their peaks jagged with scorn,
Each ridge, a silent witness to the grief she's always borne.
Abandoned at her birth, his love a fleeting, fragile spark,
He left to shield her from his curse, yet left her in the dark.
Her past, a tangled bramble, not her fault, yet sharp with blame,
Each memory, a thorn that carves her soul, whispering her name.
The townsfolk spit their venom, call her wicked, call her strange,
Hated by the many, their fear a cage they'd rearrange.
Yet some, the quiet few, leave offerings at her door,
A loaf, a sprig of sage, a kindness she can't ignore.
Their love, a fragile tether, holds her heart from breaking quite,
But cannot still the trembling in the watches of the night.
The cursed river murmurs, its waters black and sly,
It slithers through the valley, singing secrets that won't die.
Its ripples taunt her dreams, a mirror to her pain,
Reflecting every wound, each loss, like echoes of a chain.
The mountain creatures stalk her, their eyes like embers glow,
Claws scrape the shadowed pines, their whispers cruel and low.
They know her father's sins, they scent her fragile dread,
Their hunger weaves a nightmare from the stories in her head.
Alone, she weaves her spells, her fingers deft with fear,

Each charm a fleeting armor 'gainst the darkness drawing near.

The wind howls through the hollows, a dirge for what's been lost,

Her father's death, a weight, her loneliness, its cost.

Tormented by a past she never chose, she stands,

A witch of grit and sorrow, with magic in her hands.

The river hums, the creatures creep, the townsfolk turn away,

Yet in her heart, a fire burns, to face another day.

PURSUED

At the age of 63 my silver hair fell in loose waves down my back and in my eyes you could see the wisdom of an old lady who for decades had been a witch shadowed by her past, tethered to a curse born not of my own making, but of my family. My father was a good man and preacher but he had special blessings, gifts, that set the townsfolk trembling against him. The very gifts that were meant for healing and guidance, were feared as devilry, and I, his only child, bore the weight of that suspicion. When father died, the curse that bound me shattered and I was no longer pursued by it. I was free. His death was no tragedy but a release, a final sermon of love that set our spirits free. The townspeople who once raised their voices and yelled, "witch", with venom, now nodded to me in the streets with respect. The river, once a cursed serpent that hissed my father's sins at me and that of my family lineage, now flowed clear and no longer stalked or pursued me in my dreams. The mountain creatures-clawed the shadows, and ember-eyed watchers retreated into deep woods, their hunger for me no longer present. I was free. unburdened.

I made mountain herbs, charms, scented soaps of lavender and pine that I sold at the market. My reputation as a healer, praised openly. There were no longer any forced smiles, just genuine hearts of friendship and inclusion. I was tying up some dried rosemary when it caught the eye of a woman. I gestured to her to see if she was interested in a purchase when her daughter caught my eye. A little child with auburn hair and eyes the color of the sky, so light colored blue you could see the blackness of her pupil. That child's eyes stopped me cold. The child had the "gift."

As the woman approached me I said to her, "Good mornin', ma'am. Your girl. She's special ain't she?" The woman startled, tightened her grip around her child's hand. "She's just lively, loves the river and the woods, always wandering."

"Mind her close now. Those woods, that river, they're alive in ways most can't see. Her eyes, they hold the gift. The mountains will notice. Creatures too. They'll sense her, same as they sensed me once."

The woman frowned uneasily. "What are you saying? She is just a child,"

"I'm saying she's got power in her, whether you name it or not. The river can whisper things, pull her close. The woods hide things that ain't always kind. Teach her to listen but not to trust too easily. Keep her from wandering alone until she is old enough to know her strength."

The little girl's eyes were fixated on me. She understood more than her mother did.

I slipped a small talisman—a smooth stone etched with a protective rune—into the child's hand. "Keep this, little one. It'll hum if the shadows get too close."

The mother hesitated, then nodded, tucking the stone into her pocket. "Thank you, Miss Dee. I'll... I'll watch her."

As they walked away, the girl glanced back, her sky-eyes catching the sun, and I felt a stir of memory—my own childhood, my mother's warnings, the weight of a gift both beautiful and perilous.

But I was free now, my past no longer a chain. I turned back to my stall, the mountain breeze cool on my face, and continued my work, a witch at peace, tethered only to the life I chose. Free of pursuit.

GNATS AND FLIES

In the Appalachian folds, where ancient ridges hum,
The air grows thick, a restless thrum.
Gnats and flies, in swarms they rise,
A buzzing veil beneath gray skies.
Their wings, a whisper, soft yet dire,
Like omens kindled by some unseen fire.
The trails are choked with their frenzied dance,
A plague of wings in a fleeting trance.
From laurel thickets to hickory shade,
Their hum foretells what the hills evade.
A vinegar tang, sharp and sour,
Clings to the breeze in the evening hour.
It's not just scent, nor insects' flight,
But something deeper, a creeping blight.
The mountains know, in their stoic way,
Of shadows looming, of fates that sway.
Each gnat's small dart, each fly's low drone,
Sings of a future not yet shown.
The old folks pause, their eyes grow dim,
They smell the air and chant the hymn:
"When gnats arise and vinegar stings,
The hills forewarn of wretched things."
A storm, a loss, or a wound unseen,
The signs converge where the ridges lean.
In hollows deep, where the mists abide,
The flies and gnats weave a fateful tide.
Their ceaseless buzz, a harbinger's call,
A warning etched in the mountain's thrall.
The vinegar burns, the air grows tight,
The Appalachians brace for the coming night.

ANCIENTS

In the Appalachian crags, where shadows weave,
The Ancients dwell, their watch they keep.
Silent guardians, carved of stone and time,
Rooted deep in spruce and pine.
Their eyes, unseen, hold secrets vast,
Binding present to the mountain's past.
They cradle the towns, these hamlets small,
Where mist and memory softly fall.
In cobbled streets and firelight's glow,
They shield the folk from winds that blow.
No name they bear, no form they claim,
Yet every heart feels their quiet flame.
Among the people, a girl does roam,
Eyes like the sky where wild hawks soar.
Clear as the blue of a dawn's first light,
Her gaze pierces through the veil of night.
A witch, they whisper, with gifts divine,
Her hands mend wounds, her dreams align.
She walks the ridges where the Ancients sleep,
Her steps a vow, her secrets deep.
With herbs and chants, she heals the frail,
Her visions part the coming veil.
The future speaks in her quiet trance,

A glimpse of fate in her sky-blue glance.

The Ancients know her, this child of grace,

Her power, a thread in the mountain's lace.

They guide her path through fern and stone,

Ensuring she's never left alone.

For she's their voice, their chosen kin,

To guard the hills from the dark within.

In moonlit hollows, her songs take flight,

A witch's heart in the star-strewn night.

The townsfolk trust her, though some may fear,

Her blue eyes gleam when the storm draws near.

With Ancients' blessing, she holds the line,

This sky-eyed girl, both healer and divine.

In the Appalachian hills, where whispers cling to stone,
A little girl with sky-blue eyes wanders paths alone.
Her laughter dances with the breeze, through hemlock and through
     pine,
Unknowing of the sacred spark, her spirit's light divine.
Her eyes, like pools of morning sky, reflect the world's soft grace,
Yet hold a power, deep and still, no mortal heart can trace.
The Ancestors, in timeless watch, their ancient vigil keep,
Their silent strength enfolds her close, in daylight and in sleep.
She skips through glades where wildflowers bloom, her footsteps
     soft and free,
Unaware the mountain's pulse hums low in harmony.
The Ancients bless her tender soul, though she knows not their care,
Their whispers weave through misty air, a shield forever there.
When shadows creep through hollows deep, or storms begin to wail,
Their unseen hands guide her small frame along the rugged trail.
No harm may touch this child of light, her blue eyes bright and clear,
For she's the kin of mountain gods, though she does not yet hear.
She dreams of stars, of rivers wide, of secrets in the glen,
Not knowing that her gentle heart holds magic older than men.
The Ancestors smile, their will unseen, as she plays beneath their
     gaze,
This blessed girl, with sky-blue eyes, will shine through all her days.

PRECEDENT TO PLEAD

In the Appalachian heart, where mountains hum and sway,
A precedent is pleaded, 'neath the sky's eternal gray.
A little girl, a witchling born, with eyes like azure flame,
Blessed by powers deep and old, though she knows not her name.
The river runs, a silver vein, through valleys green and wide,
Its waters sing of life and death, where secrets still abide.
The townsfolk gather, hushed and wary, by the fire's trembling light,
They speak of her, the sky-eyed child, who mends the broken night.
Her hands weave spells she doesn't ken, with herbs and whispered
    lore,
Healing wounds and hearts alike, as Ancients did before.
The cryptids roam the shadowed woods—Mothman's wings, a
    fleeting blur,
The Wampus Cat, with amber eyes, keeps watch o'er her and her.
The forest breathes with life's own pulse, yet death is never far,
Each leaf that falls, each bone that rests, beneath the evening star.
The girl, she walks where willows weep, her steps a sacred plea,
For balance held 'twixt light and dark, in mountain's mystery.
The townsfolk lean on her young grace, though fear her gifts as well,
For power in a child's small frame stirs tales they dare not tell.
Yet Ancestors, in mist and stone, stand guard with timeless might,
Their blessing shields her fragile form from perils of the night.
The river speaks of cycles old, of birth and death's embrace,
While cryptids stalk the twilight's edge, their eyes on her sweet face.
She is their hope, their precedent, to hold the world aright,
A witch, a girl, with sky-blue eyes, the keeper of the light.
In Appalachia's ancient arms, where life and death entwine,
She pleads through acts of love and care, her powers pure, divine.
The mountains watch, the cryptids glide, the river's song endures,
This blessed child, their sacred charge, forever will be hers.

CRYPTIC

In the folds of Appalachia's ancient green,

Where mist and mountain weave a dream unseen,

A cryptic child, with hair like woven bark,

Treads soft through hollows, lit by starlight's spark.

Her eyes, clear blue as skies before the rain,

Hold secrets deep, where mysteries remain.

Within her left eye, faint, a crescent gleams,

A birthmark traced in moonlight's silver beams.

So slight, it hides, yet pulses with a grace,

A mark of witches, blessed by sacred space.

The Ancients, too, have kissed her azure sight,

Divine their touch, eternal as the night.

She knows not yet the power she's been given,

This child of earth, by mountain spirits driven.

The ridges whisper, soft as rivers flow,

Of destinies the cryptic girl will know.

Her gaze, a portal, sees what none may see—

The threads of fate, the world's old sorcery.

Through laurel thickets, where the shadows play,

The Wampus Cat keeps watch, both night and day.

Mothman's wings, a flicker in the gloom,

Guard her small form beneath the silver moon.

The witches' blessing, woven at her birth,

Binds her to the soul of this old earth.

The townsfolk speak in hushed and reverent tones,

Of her blue eyes, of crescent carved in stone.

They see her heal with hands too young to know,

The magic deep in her spirit grows.

Yet she, this child, with laughter light and free,

Feels only joy in stream and ancient tree.

O cryptic girl, with birthmark soft and bright,

Your eyes hold stars that guide the mountain's night.

The divine and witches, in their timeless lore,

Have marked you theirs, to wander evermore.

In Appalachia's heart, your blue gaze sings,

Of sacred truths and all the coming springs.

DISTANT WOODS

In the heart of the Appalachian woods,
where shadows weave through ancient pine,
the distant hollers hum with secrets,
their whispers sharp, their cadence fine.
Beneath a canopy of starlit green,
where moss clings soft to weathered stone,
a little girl with clear sky-blue eyes
treads paths where wild things roam alone.
Her eyes, twin pools of boundless azure,
hold flecks of starlight, strange and bright—
a birthmark gleams, a cosmic sigil,
etched by forces old as night.
The creatures stir, both seen and hidden,
from shadowed vale to misty ridge:
the bobcat's prowl, the owl's low murmur,
the skittering steps on a twig-strewn bridge.
The cryptids call, their voices eerie—
Mothman's wings hum soft and dire,
Bigfoot's tread shakes roots asunder,
Wampus Cat glints with eyes of fire.
Aliens, too, from realms uncharted,
their silver craft in moon-glow veiled,
sing through the ether, soft vibrations,
to the girl whose fate the stars have hailed.

The rivers churn with ancient bloodlines,

their currents pulse with primal might.

The land itself, with breath of granite,

knows her step, her will, her light.

The witch-to-be, with eyes like heaven,

bears the mark of earth and sky,

linked to all—the beast, the spirit,

the unseen worlds that never die.

The whippoorwill cries out her coming,

the fireflies dance to name her queen.

The wind weaves spells through sycamore branches,

its song a vow to the yet unseen.

One day she'll rule these rugged mountains,

her voice a thread through stream and stone,

the Appalachian heart her kingdom,

its creatures hers, their blood her own.

For now, she listens, small and silent,

as woods and distant voices call,

the girl with sky-blue eyes and birthmark,

destined to bind and rule them all.

UPON THE DISTANT WATERS

Upon the distant waters, where the Appalachian rivers sing,
Their currents weave through ancient stone, a restless, living thing,
An old witch, Charlotta Dee, now seventy winters strong,
Watched a girl with sky-blue eyes, her soul as clear as dawn.
A birthmark gleamed within her gaze, a star-flecked, mystic sign,
Tying Rose to the mountain's heart, to river, root, and vine.
Charlotta, gnarled as blackthorn, with secrets carved in bone,
Saw the spark in little Rose, a power yet unknown.
With her mother's nod, she took the child beneath her weathered
      wing,
Taught her spells in moonlit glades, where wildwood spirits cling.
The old ways bloomed in whispered chants, in herbs and starlit
      streams,
In runes etched deep in river rock, in dreams that pierced the seams.
The forest watched, its creatures near—the owl with amber stare,
The cryptids, veiled in twilight's hush, their murmurs filled the air.
Mothman's wings brushed soft as mist, the Wampus Cat prowled
      low,
The dead, in spectral council, wove their will through winds that
      blow.
The river sang of ancient pacts, its waters cold and wise,
And Rose, with birthmark in her eyes, was bound to all that lies.
"Swear to me," old Charlotta said, her voice like cracking stone,
"Never leave this mountain's heart, this land you call your own.

A contract sealed with earth and blood, with spirits, shade, and
    stream,
To guard the woods, the cryptids' call, the dead's eternal dream."
Rose, with eyes like boundless sky, gave her vow beneath the stars,
Her heart entwined with ridge and root, her soul unmarked by scars.
The river roared its fierce approval, the forest hummed its trust,
The cryptids bowed, the spirits sighed, the dead rose from their dust.
Charlotta Dee, her task complete, stood tall by water's edge,
Her eyes on Rose, the child of fate, now bound by sacred pledge.
Upon the distant waters' flow, the mountain's will would stand,
Through Rose, its queen, forever tied to river, soul, and land.

PEEPING AT MORN

At morn's first blush, where mist clings low,

Charlotta Dee, now frail and slow,

Peeps through the haze, her eyes grown dim,

In late-seventies' waning hymn.

The Appalachian dawn unfolds,

Its secrets whispered, fierce and old.

She watches Rose, the witch-girl small,

With clear sky-blue eyes that see it all—

A birthmark gleams, a starry trace,

Binding her soul to this wild place.

The land leans close, its breath alive,

The pines sway soft, the rivers strive.

The bobcat pauses, eyes aglow,

The cryptids hum where shadows flow.

Mothman's wings graze Rose's path,

The Wampus Cat stalks, fierce with wrath.

The forest spirits weave her name,

The dead, half-seen, stake silent claim.

The river, gleaming, cold, and sly,

Watches Rose with a jealous eye.

But then a whisper, sharp with dread,

Breaks through the morn—news of the dead.

A girl-child drowned in the river's maw,

Her small life claimed by ancient law.

The waters took her, swift and cruel,

An offering seized in the swirling pool.

The river, thwarted, could not take Rose,

Yet hungers still where its current flows.

Its appetite stirs, the cycle spins,

A dance of loss where fate begins.

Charlotta, weak, her magic spent,

Her body bowed, her spirit bent,

Feels her mind fray, a fading thread,

Yet clings to warnings left unsaid.

"Rose," she croaks, her voice a rasp,

"Beware the river's greedy grasp.

The land, it loves you, but it craves,

Its roots entwine with ancient graves.

The dead will call, their voices thin,

To steal your soul, to pull you in."

Rose, with eyes like boundless sky,

Hears the words, her heart held high.

The birthmark pulses, a mystic sign,

Her fate entwined with ridge and vine.

The river sings, its waters gleam,

A siren's call, a deadly dream.

Charlotta, fading, grips her hand,

"Stay wary, child, of this wild land.

The river wants you for its own,

To claim your heart, your blood, your bone."

The morning hums, the spirits sigh,

The cryptids watch with knowing eye.

The dead still linger, cold and near,

Their whispers sharp with want and fear.

Rose stands tall, though danger calls,

Her soul a flame where twilight falls.

The river waits, its hunger deep,

While Charlotta's warnings softly weep.

A CIRCLE DIVIDED

In the heart of the Appalachians, where the mountains claw the sky,
A circle splits the shadowed land, where whispers never die.
By the river's restless murmur, cold and silver in its flow,
A girl child met her end, where the wild things come and go.
Her laughter once had danced there, through the laurel's tangled
green,
Chasing fireflies at twilight, in a world half-unseen.
But the current claimed her softly, in its dark and greedy pull,
And the mountains stood in silence, as her light faded full.
Good and evil walk these ridges, side by side, they weave,
In the hearts of mountain people, in the stories they believe.
The preacher's voice is fervent, calling grace from rocky ground,
Yet the moonshine stills burn quiet, where the law's not often found.
A mother hums a hymn at dawn, her hands worn by the plow,
While a hunter's rage lies smoldering, no one dares to question how.
The river carries secrets, of both kindness and of sin,
In these hills, the line's a shadow, where the two worlds blend
within.
The circle holds them tightly—good and evil, intertwined,
In the cedar smoke and starlight, in the roots of ancient pine.
Her spirit haunts the water's edge, a flicker in the spray,
A reminder of the balance that the mountains hold always.
For every hand that heals here, there's a fist that strikes in spite,
Every prayer meets whispered curses in the hollows of the night.

In the Appalachians' circle, where the river sings her name,
Good and evil share the silence, neither one will bear the blame.

DISTURBED SLOPES OF HILLS

In the Appalachian folds, where hills wear scars like veins,
Disturbed slopes crumble softly, torn by time and heavy rains.
Charlotta Dee, now eighty, treads these paths with faltering feet,
Her memory is a fading ember, lost in mist where shadows meet.
Once she knew each ridge and hollow, every bend of stream and
    stone,
Named the wildflowers in springtime, claimed these mountains as
her own.
But now the names slip through her, like water through a sieve,
Her mind is a fog-bound valley, where the past no longer lives.
Her body bends like weathered pines, illness carving slow and deep,
Each breath a labor, heavy, as the hills themselves might weep.
The slopes, churned by man's ambition, mirror her unmoored
    decline,
Their roots are exposed, unstable, like her thoughts that intertwine.
She forgets the songs of sparrows, the taste of blackberry wine,
The faces of her kinfolk, blurred beneath the weight of time.
Yet sometimes, in the twilight, a flicker sparks within her eyes,
A glimpse of girlhood summers, chasing fireflies in the skies.
The mountains, scarred and silent, hold her in their ancient sway,
Their disturbed earth is a witness to the life that slips away.
Charlotta Dee is fading, like the hills that bear the cost,
Of time's relentless carving, of the things forever lost.
Good and evil, love and sorrow, linger in these ridges still,

Side by side, they cradle her, on this slow-dying hill.

As Charlotta's breath grows thinner, the mountains hum her name,
A requiem for broken slopes, for a soul that's not the same.

BORN OF CHAINS AND MOODS

In the heart of Appalachia's ancient folds,
Where mountains whisper tales untold,
Lived Charlotta Dee, a witch of lore,
Born of chains, her spirit sore.
Her middle eighties carved in stone,
She walked the ridges, never alone—
With shadows dancing, moods that swayed,
The old ways in her blood were laid.
Born where the hollers cradle the night,
Under stars that burned with ghostly light,
Charlotta wove her spells in quiet,
Her voice is a thread through death's disquiet.
The spirits answered, soft and near,
Their secrets only she could hear.
Her hands, gnarled as the oak's old bark,
Kindled magic in the mountain's dark.
By her side, a girl with eyes like skies,
Clear and blue, where starlight lies.
A little witch, her heart unbound,
Drank the wisdom from the sacred ground.
Charlotta taught her chants and signs,
The roots, the bones, the woven vines,
To speak with those who've crossed the veil,
To read the wind, to never fail.
In her cabin, smoke and herbs would rise,
As Charlotta's voice pierced clouded skies.
"Child," she'd say, "the dead don't rest,
They linger here, in earth's own chest.
Listen close, their truths are cold,
But hold the warmth of stories old."
The girl, with eyes like morning's dew,
Learned the craft, her power grew.
When Charlotta's breath began to fade,
In the mountains where her life was made,

She called the girl, her voice a sigh,
"Carry on when I must lie."
The witch's heart, so fierce, so worn,
Slipped to shadows 'fore the morn.
Her death a ripple through the glen,
The spirits mourned their oldest friend.
Now the girl, with clear sky-blue eyes,
Walks the paths where Charlotta lies.
The gifted one, she talks to those
Whose whispers linger in the throes.
The chains are gone, the moods still sway,
The old ways live, they'll never fray.
In Appalachian night, her voice ascends,
The witch's craft, it never ends.

SOLITUDE

Rose knelt by the hearth in Charlotta Dee's cabin, the firelight casting shadows that danced like restless spirits across the worn pine walls. The air smelled of sage and damp earth, a scent that clung to the old witch's home even now, weeks after her passing. Rose's fingers traced the carvings on the mantel—runes Charlotta had etched decades ago, wards against the things that stirred in the Appalachian night. The cabin was silent, save for the distant roar of the river, a sound that followed Rose into her dreams, mingling with the whispers of cryptids, the hum of something not of this world, and the murmurs of the dead who lingered in the hollows.

She was alone, though not entirely. Back at her parents' home, a mile down the mountain, her mother and father went about their days—her mother tending the herb garden, her father splitting wood with the same quiet rhythm he'd kept since Rose was a girl. They loved her, but they didn't *see* her, not the way Charlotta had. Her mentor had understood the weight of Rose's gift, the way the mountain spoke to her, its voice a chorus of wind and root and bone. Now, without Charlotta, Rose felt like a thread pulled loose from the weave of the world.

She came to the cabin often, sometimes staying for days. Her parents didn't question it; they knew she was Charlotta's heir, bound to the mountain by a promise made when she was seven. Rose could still see herself, small and wide-eyed, kneeling beside Charlotta under a sky bruised with storm clouds. "You'll stay, child," Charlotta had said, her voice like gravel and honey. "The mountain needs a keeper, a conduit for its secrets. Swear it." Rose had sworn, her hand pressed to the earth, feeling its pulse answer her own.

Now, a young woman, that promise felt like a chain. Rose stood, brushing ash from her skirt, and stepped outside. The night was alive, the air sharp with pine and the faint, electric tang of something *other*. The mountain was never quiet. She heard the low, mournful call of a creature that wasn't deer or bear, a cryptid skulking in the shadows. Somewhere beyond the ridge, a light flickered—not a star, but something that watched. And beneath it all, the dead whispered, their voices threading through the roots, telling stories of lost travelers and forgotten wars. Rose closed her eyes, letting the mountain's pulse steady her own. She was its keeper, its voice, but tonight she felt like a stranger in its embrace.

She thought of leaving. The world beyond the Appalachians called to her in fleeting moments—cities with their bright lights, lives where she might be more than a witch bound to stone and shadow. She could study, love, and build something new. But the promise held her fast. Charlotta had warned her: "Leave, and the mountain's secrets spill out. The balance breaks. You're the conduit, Rose. Without you, the dead walk, the cryptids hunt unchecked, and the things from the stars grow bold."

Rose walked to the river, its roar louder now, a wild hymn that drowned out her doubts. She sat on a moss-covered rock, her boots brushing the water's edge. In her dreams, the river was Charlotta's voice, guiding her through rituals and warnings. Last night, she'd dreamed of a figure in the mist, not Charlotta, but something older, its eyes like polished obsidian, beckoning her deeper into the woods. She'd woken with her heart pounding, the taste of iron in her mouth.

Her parents didn't understand. They were of the mountain, but not *in* it, not the way Rose was. Her mother would smile and say, "You're young, Rose. You'll find your way." Her father would nod, his hands busy with axe or rope, as if her solitude was just a phase. But it wasn't. It was a hollow ache, a space Charlotta had once filled with stories and spells, with the certainty that Rose's purpose was enough.

She stayed at the cabin that night, curled under Charlotta's quilt, the river's song seeping into her bones. In the dark, she felt the mountain watching, waiting. The cryptids' calls grew sharper, the aliens' hum closer, the dead's whispers more insistent. They knew her, needed her. She was their keeper, their conduit, bound by a child's oath and a witch's duty.

By morning, the thought of leaving felt like a betrayal. Rose stood at the cabin's threshold, her breath visible in the dawn chill. The mountain stretched before her, vast and ancient, its secrets hers to carry. She thought of Charlotta's weathered hands, her fierce eyes, the way she'd called Rose "daughter of the ridge." The loneliness didn't lift, but it settled, a familiar weight. Rose stepped back inside, lit the fire, and began the day's work—brewing potions, tending wards, listening to the mountain's endless song.

She would stay. Not because she wanted to, but because she was all the mountain had.

THE TANGLED MASS OF WILL AND FATE

In the Appalachian heart, where shadows weave,
Rose, the witch, young and fair, does grieve.
Her beauty glows like moonlit fern and stone,
Yet bound to crags, she wanders not alone.
The mountain hums, a pulse beneath her feet,
Its roots entwine her soul, her fate complete.
A child's oath, sworn to earth and shade,
Ties her to rivers where wild voices wade.
She dreams of cities, lights that pierce the sky,
Of lives unbound, where wings of will might fly.
A love to hold, a hand to call her own,
Beyond the ridge, where heartbeats aren't of stone.
But fate, a tangled mass, denies her flight,
Its threads are woven with the mountain's might.
The river roars, her lover and her chain,
Its endless song her solace and her pain.
Cryptids call, their cries a shadowed plea,
Aliens hum where starlight bends the tree.
The dead whisper secrets, cold and near,
And Rose, their conduit, is bound to hear.
Her heart, an ember bright with fleeting fire,
Burns for a world beyond the granite spire.
Yet love, like water, slips through longing's grasp,
Her fate decrees the river's endless clasp.

No suitor's touch, no mortal's vow can stay,

The mountain claims her, night by starlit day.

In solitude, her will and fate entwine,

A witch of beauty, bound to ridge and rhyme.

O Rose, the keeper, lovely, lone, and still,

The Appalachians hold your heart, your will.

The river sings, your only bride to be,

In a tangled mass of fate, you're never free.

THE DEBATABLE SOUL

In the heart of the Appalachians, where the peaks kiss the sky, Lived Rose, the mountain witch, with a spark in her eye. Her hands wove the old magic, her roots deep in the stone, Bound by an oath to the ridges, she'd never leave them alone.

Desi Johnson, a doctor, came striding through the mist, With a stethoscope and a city heart, his logic tightly fixed. He tended Rose's mother, struck by fever from a fall. In her cabin's dim-lit glow, he answered healing's call.

Her parents sang his praises, their gratitude sincere, For Desi's skill had chased the shadow of their fear. But Rose, oh, she was wildfire, her spirit fierce and free, And Desi's heart, unmoored, fell hard for her mystery.

He saw her in the moonlight, chanting by the stream, Her voice a thread of magic, unraveling his dreams. "I love you, Rose," he whispered, his soul alight with flame, But her eyes grew sharp as quartz when her answer came.

"I'm bound to these old mountains, by an oath I swore to keep. My heart's tied to the ridges, where the ancient spirits sleep. I cannot leave, not ever, though my love for you is true, The mountains are my marrow—there's nothing I can do."

Desi laughed, a city scoff, "An oath? That's childish lore! You'd chain yourself to stone and myth? There's a world to explore!" His words, like careless arrows, pierced her proud, unyielding soul, Rose's gaze turned cold as winter, her voice a bitter toll.

"You mock what holds me sacred, you scorn what makes me whole. Respect's the price of love, Desi, or you've no claim to my soul. Leave now, and speak no more to me—your heart's too small to see." She turned, her shadow fading into the mountain's lee.

Desi stood, his heart a storm, torn by love and pride, The witch of the Appalachians had stirred a war inside. Could he bend, embrace her world, her oath, her sacred ground? Or would he walk away, forever city-bound?

Her parents' warmth still lingered, their trust in him profound, Yet Rose's final words left echoes all around. He loved her fierce, unyielding heart, but could he understand? The mountains held her soul, as they held her oath's command.

In the silence of the ridges, Desi's soul debates alone, To chase a love that's wild and true, or let it turn to stone. For Rose, the witch of starlight, would never leave her throne, And love, without respect, is just a seed unsown.

SWEET ASSURANCES

The mist clung to the Appalachian peaks like a lover's breath, curling through the pines and settling over Rose's cabin. The air was thick with the scent of damp earth and wild honeysuckle, and the moon hung low, silvering the world below. Rose, the witch of the mountains, stood on her porch, her hair spilling over her shoulders. Her hands, calloused from years of gathering herbs and weaving spells, gripped the railing as she stared out at the endless ridges. She was as fierce as the storms that raked these peaks, and bound by an oath to never leave the mountains—a vow sworn to the spirits that guarded her kin.

Desi Johnson, stood a few paces away, his doctor's bag slung over one shoulder, his city-bred boots sinking slightly into the soft earth. He'd come to these mountains a month ago to tend to Rose's mother, who'd taken a fever after a fall. A traveling doctor if you will. He went where he was needed the most. The infection was gone now, thanks to his careful hands, but something else had taken root in him—a love for Rose, fierce and unyielding, that had bloomed in the quiet moments of their talks by the hearth. Her sharp wit, her stories of the mountain spirits, the way her eyes caught the firelight—it had all undone him.

Tonight, he'd come to confess it. But Rose had spoken first, her voice steady as granite. "I love you, Desi," she'd said, her gaze unflinching. "But I'm bound here. This mountain's my blood, my bone. I swore an oath to the spirits when I was sixteen, to protect this place and never leave. I can't go with you, not to your city, not anywhere."

Desi's heart had lurched, not with surprise but with a pang of longing. He'd known she was tethered to this place—her parents had hinted at it, their faces warm with pride for their daughter's strength. But hearing it from her lips, so final, so fierce, had stirred something in him. He could leave, return to his world of sterile clinics and bustling streets. But could he leave her?

He stepped closer, his breath visible in the cool night air. "Rose," he said softly, his voice carrying the gentle cadence of his Southern roots, "I don't care if you're bound to this mountain. I don't care if you never step foot in a city or see the ocean. You're in my heart now, and that's a place you'll never leave."

She turned, her eyes narrowing, searching for mockery. She'd heard men laugh before, dismissing her oath as superstition, her life as small. But Desi's face was open, his brown eyes steady, his hands outstretched but not reaching, giving her space. "You don't understand," she said, her voice sharp. "This isn't a choice. The spirits hold me here. If I leave, I break my word, and the mountain—my home, my people— pays the price. You'll tire of this place, Desi. You'll want more."

He shook his head, a small smile tugging at his lips. "Rose, you're more than any city could ever be. You're starlight and storm, magic and bone. I've seen you coax life from herbs, heard you sing to the wind like it listens. You think I'd trade that for concrete and noise?" He took a step closer, his voice dropping to a whisper. "I love you, Rose. Not for what you might be somewhere else, but for who you are right here, right now. If you're bound to this mountain, then I'll carry it in my heart too."

Her throat tightened. She'd expected him to argue, to scoff like others had, to call her oath foolish and walk away. But Desi's words were like a balm, soothing the raw edges of her fear. Still, doubt lingered. "You'll leave, Desi," she said, softer now, almost a plea. "Your life's out there—hospitals, cities, a world I'll never touch. You'll forget me." He closed the distance between them, stopping just short of the porch steps. "Never," he said, his voice firm but tender. "If I leave, I'll carry you with me. Every time I see a ridge against the sky, I'll see your silhouette. Every time I smell pine or hear a stream, I'll hear your voice. You're not just a moment, Rose. You're my forever, whether I'm here or a thousand miles away."

Tears pricked her eyes, but she blinked them back, her pride as unyielding as the granite beneath her feet. "And if you stay?" she asked, her voice barely above a whisper. "What then? This mountain's no easy place. It's wild, it's hard, and I'm no gentle woman."

Desi's smile widened, warm as the hearthfire she loved. "Then I'll learn about the mountain, Rose. I'll learn its ways, its spirits, its heart. I'll learn you. And if I can't stay forever, if life pulls me away, I'll come back. Always. You're my home now, oath or no oath."

For a moment, silence held them, the mountain itself seeming to listen. Rose stepped down from the porch, her bare feet silent on the earth. She stopped inches from him, searching his face. "You mean it," she said, not a question but a realization.

"With every breath," he replied.

She reached out, her fingers brushing his, tentative at first, then firm. "Then love me here, Desi. Love me as I am, mountain and all. And if you go, keep your promise. Carry me in your heart."

He took her hand, his grip warm and sure. "Always, Rose. Always."

Under the watchful moon, with the mountains as their witness, they stood together, two souls bound not by oaths but by something deeper—a love that could span ridges and cities, rooted in the wild heart of the Appalachians.

A WEARY CIRCUIT

In the heart of Appalachia, where ridges hum low,
A weary circuit winds through valleys aglow.
Copper veins pulse, frayed by time's heavy hand,
Yet tethered to love, rooted deep in the land.
She stands like the mountain, steadfast, unswayed,
Her eyes hold the starlight that never will fade.
He kneels in the shadow of pine and of stone,
Pledging his heart to their wild, sacred home.
"Never shall I wander," he swears to the peak,
Her hand in his, steady, no words need they speak.
The circuit may falter, its wires worn thin,
But their vow burns eternal, no spark lost within.
Through seasons of frost and of fire's warm bloom,
Their love is the current that banishes gloom.
No short in the line, no break in the flow,
Bound to the mountain, their spirits will grow.
The circuit may tire, yet it carries their creed,
A love that won't flicker, a home they won't leave.
In Appalachia's embrace, their pledge shall endure,
A flame in the wire, forever secure.

WARNING SIGNS

In the hollows of Appalachia, where whispers weave through pine,
Victoria watches, her heart a tangled, jealous vine.
Her love for Doctor Desi burns, a fever fierce and wild,
Yet Rose, the mountain witch, holds his heart, serene and beguiled.
Her eyes, sharp as flint, catch every glance he spares,
Each smile Desi gives to Rose ignites her envious flares.
She paces in the moonlight, her thoughts a shadowed snare,
Plotting ways to sever the bond that blooms so fair.
Her laughter cracks like thunder, too loud, too forced, too shrill,
A mask to hide the venom that her heart cannot conceal.
She lingers near his clinic, her gifts of herbs and wine,
Laced with subtle pleas, "Choose me, leave Rose's mystic shrine."
Her words drip honeyed poison, sowing doubt in quiet tones,
"She's wild, that witch of ridges, she'll bind you to the stones."
Victoria's fingers tremble, weaving plans to break their tie,
Her love a twisted current, sparking warnings in the sky.
She carves his name in cedar, whispers charms to steal his will,
Her jealousy a storm that gathers, darkening the hill.
Yet Rose's magic holds him, her roots too deep to rend,
And Victoria's schemes falter, her heart cursed to descend.
Beware the signs of envy, her smile that cuts like glass,
The frantic need to fracture love that's destined to surpass.
For Victoria, love's captive, her longing turns to spite,
A jealous flame that burns alone in Appalachia's night.

WHITE ROSES

In the folds of the Appalachian Mountains, where mist clings to the ridges like a lover's breath, Victoria lived in a clapboard house nestled among fields of corn and wildflowers. She was a vision, with hair like raven's wings and eyes that caught the dawn's first light. Her parents, teachers by day and farmers by dusk, tilled the earth and sowed lessons of hard work and faith. Victoria, their only child, carried their hopes like a basket of fresh-picked apples, heavy but sweet.

On a Sunday afternoon, the air thick with summer and hymns, Victoria stepped into the small wooden church in town. She carried a bundle of white roses, their petals soft as a prayer, and placed them on the altar beneath the cross. The sunlight streamed through stained glass, painting her in hues of gold and crimson. That's when Desi saw her. He sat in the back pew, his doctor's hands folded, his heart tethered to Rose, the woman whose laughter was like the ripple of a mountain stream. But Victoria—her grace, the way her fingers lingered on the flowers—stirred something in him, a spark he couldn't name.

Desi, lean and kind-eyed, was new to the hollow, a city-trained physician who'd come to mend the ailments of these hills. Rose, an Appalachian witch with a gift for herbs and omens, had claimed his heart months ago. Their love was quiet, steady, like the roots of an old oak. Yet, as he watched Victoria sway softly to the organ's hum, her beauty was a melody he couldn't unhear. He left the church with Rose in his heart, her hand in his, but Victoria lingered in his mind like a shadow that wouldn't fade.

Victoria, though, felt no such restraint. The moment Desi's gaze met hers, a fire kindled in her chest. His warm brown eyes, the way he tipped his hat with a shy smile—she was undone. Love, instant and fierce, sank its claws into her. She didn't know Rose, not really, only that she was the woman who walked beside Desi, her braids woven with sage and her presence like a spell. Victoria didn't care. She wanted him, and she'd have him. She whispered to herself under the stars that night, "I'll make him mine. Rose be damned."

Days turned to weeks, and Victoria's longing grew sharp as a briar. She found excuses to visit Desi's clinic, bringing jars of her mother's preserves or asking about a cough she didn't have. Each time, his kindness was a blade, cutting deeper because it wasn't hers alone. She watched him with Rose at the market, their easy laughter a wound she nursed in secret. At night, she'd sit by her window, sketching his face in her mind, vowing to unravel the thread that bound him to the witch. One moonless night, as thunder rumbled over the peaks, Victoria woke with a start. Her room was cold, the air heavy with the scent of damp earth and something older, like decayed leaves. At the foot of her bed stood a figure, gnarled and translucent, her eyes like twin coals in a withered face. It was Charlotta Dee, the old witch who'd lived deep in the holler, dead these past ten years. Her voice was a rasp, like wind through dry branches. "Leave him be, girl," she hissed. "What's sacred, you don't touch. What God has joined, you don't tear asunder."

Victoria's heart pounded, but her jaw set firm. "He's not hers forever," she whispered, defiant. Charlotta's form flickered, her finger pointing like a curse. "You'll bring ruin, child. Heed the warning." The vision dissolved, leaving Victoria trembling, her sheets damp with sweat. She told herself it was a dream, a trick of the mind, but Charlotta's words clung like damp moss.

The hauntings came nightly now. Charlotta's specter lingered in corners, her voice a low wail in the wind. "Sacred," she'd murmur, her eyes boring into Victoria's soul. "Joined." Victoria's resolve wavered, but her love for Desi burned hotter than fear. She began to plot in earnest—small lies whispered to neighbors, hints that Rose's remedies were more curse than cure. She left notes for Desi, unsigned, tucked under his clinic door, words of longing meant to pull him from Rose's orbit.

One evening, as Victoria walked the ridge trail, Charlotta appeared again, her form sharper, angrier. The air crackled, and the old witch's voice was a growl. "You'll break your own heart, girl, and his too. Leave what's not yours." Victoria stumbled back, her breath catching. For the first time, doubt crept in. Was her love a theft? Was Desi's heart a sacred thing, bound to Rose by something deeper than her own desire?

She stood at the edge of the field, the mountain looming dark and eternal. Desi's face haunted her, but so did Charlotta's warning. Victoria's heart was a battlefield, love and jealousy warring with the ghost's grim prophecy. She could press on, risk the ruin Charlotta foretold, or let go, leaving Desi to the witch who held him first. The mountains offered no answers, only silence, vast and unyielding, as Victoria wrestled with her soul's reckless vow.

FALCONS SNARED

In the crags of Appalachia, where falcons slice the sky,

Victoria weaves her lures, her heart a fevered lie.

Her beauty snares the air, a trap of silken guile,

Aiming for Desi's soul, with a wicked, wanton smile.

Desi, bound to Rose, feels a shadowed, sinful flame,

A lust that clouds his heart, unrequited, steeped in shame.

Victoria's eyes, like embers, call him to betray,

But the mountains watch in judgment, their verdict none can sway.

The falcons scream their warning, talons sharp with ancient lore,

"Leave the sacred bond unbroken, tempt the doctor's heart no more."

The rivers churn with fury, their currents cold and clear,

Whispering of wrath to come, should Victoria persevere.

Every creature in the hollow, from the fox to the shadowed hare,

Senses her seductive treason, feels the sin that taints the air.

The pines creak out their curses, their roots entwined with fate,

The universe itself aligns to seal her reckless hate.

Her love, a twisted hunger, seeks to rend what God has tied,

But the mountains loom eternal, their justice none can hide.

The waters roar of ruin, their torrents primed to swell,

Promising a hellish reckoning if she dares to cast her spell.

Victoria, unyielding, dances on the edge of doom,

Her heart a snare for Desi, weaving lust in twilight's gloom.

But falcons circle closer, their cries a piercing knell,

The mountains, rivers, cosmos—sworn to bring her private hell.

If she persists, the stars will dim, the earth will crack and wail,

The universe will unleash its fury, and her soul shall surely fail.

For love that's born of sin and greed, the heavens will not spare,

Victoria's fate is written—beware the falcons' glare.

WARRIOR HORSES

In the shadowed folds of Appalachia's deep,

Victoria's dreams turn dark, where nightmares creep.

Warrior horses, spawned from apocalypse's flame,

Gallop through her slumber, wild, untamed.

Their hooves spark embers, cracking earth asunder,

Eyes like blood-red stars, their whinnies thunder.

From the Book of Wrath, they ride, relentless, dire,

Heralds of a reckoning, born of cosmic fire.

Charlotta Dee, long dead, joins their spectral throng,

Her withered form a wraith, her voice a chilling song.

"Flee your wicked heart," she warns with hollowed gaze,

"Or these steeds of doom will set your soul ablaze."

Victoria twists in sleep, her mind a haunted vale,

The horses charge, their manes a storm, their breath a gale.

They hunt her through the mist, their purpose cold and clear,

To bind her to the guilt of love she dares to steer.

Charlotta's ghost points bony fingers at her sin,

"Your lust for Desi calls these harbingers within.

Their hooves will crush your schemes, their fire consume your will,

For sacred bonds defiled, the heavens seek to kill."

The mountains echo screams, the rivers boil with dread,

As warrior horses circle, trampling dreams she fed.

Victoria wakes, heart pounding, sweat upon her brow,

Charlotta's curse and equine wrath her endless torment now.

Each night they come, unyielding, through the apocalyptic haze,

The witch's shade and stallions fierce, to haunt her fleeting days.

No rest for her, no peace, while she pursues her claim,

For the horses of the end will brand her soul with flame.

A BEETLE'S PASS

In the heart of the Appalachian Mountains,
where mist clings to ridges like a lover's vow,
lies A Beetle's Pass, a shadowed cleft,
carved by time, where secrets sleep and prowl.
The peaks stand ancient, gnarled and wise,
their granite bones cloaked in hemlock green.
Whispers drift through laurel and pine,
of a cursed river, its waters unseen.
The river runs, a vein of dark lament,
beneath the Pass where beetles crawl and hum.
Its current sings of sorrow's old descent,
of folk who drank its depths and came undone.
Once, the people of this rugged land,
tended fields where wildflowers dared to bloom.
Their hands were rough, their hearts were grand,
yet the river's curse wove threads of doom.
A maiden fair, with eyes like morning dew,
loved a lad who carved his name in stone.
They swore their oaths where the wild ferns grew,
but the river claimed him, left her alone.
The land remembers—its roots entwine
with tales of loss, of fevered dreams that fade.
The beetle scuttles through the mossy shrine,
where ghosts of kin in silent vigil wade.

The cursed river twists through shale and clay,

its waters cold, a mirror to despair.

It speaks to those who wander far astray,

and bids them linger in its haunted glare.

Yet still the people toil, their spirits strong,

their cabins lit by fire's defiant glow.

They sing of hope in a weathered mountain song,

though the river's curse will never let them go.

A Beetle's Pass, where shadows softly creep,

holds the mountain's heart, both fierce and frail.

The land, the people, the river's secrets keep,

bound forever in this Appalachian tale.

NECTAR

In the folds of A Beetle's Pass, where nectar drips from wild blooms,
The Appalachian air hums soft, with love's delicate perfumes.
Desi and Rose, entwined like vines, their hearts a woven braid,
Share whispers sweet as honeysuckle, in the mountain's dappled shade.
Their love is nectar, pure and gold, a fire that warms the soul,
Born in meadows where the laurel sways, where rivers carve their toll.
Desi's laugh, a spark in twilight, Rose's touch, a tender bloom,
Together they defy the cursed river's ever-looming gloom.
But Victoria, oh, she lingers, a siren in the evening's haze,
Her eyes like embers, tempting Desi with wild, forbidden ways.
Her voice is honey, laced with thorns, her pull a dangerous art,
She stirs a longing, sharp and sweet, that tugs at Desi's heart.
Desi feels the shadow creep, yet holds Rose close with quiet grace,
Their love a shield against the lure of Victoria's fleeting face.
The town still speaks of a lover lost, a man the river claimed,
His name now moss on weathered stone, his fate forever named.
He walked the banks where willows weep, drawn by the water's call,
The cursed river, dark and deep, that swallows those who fall.
Some say he loved a girl from town, her name now lost to time,
But the river's curse, unyielding, cold, turned passion into rhyme.
Its waters churn with secrets old, beneath the mountain's watchful eye,
A warning to the lovers bold who dare its banks to lie.
Yet Desi and Rose, with nectar's glow, defy the river's claim,
Their love a flame that burns too bright to falter in its game.

Victoria's temptation fades, a flicker in the morning's light,

For Desi's heart and Rose's soul are bound beyond the night.

The river took a lover once, and grief still haunts the town,

But in A Beetle's Pass, love's nectar blooms where curses try to drown.

PURPLE

In the cradle of the Appalachian peaks,
Where purple heavens whisper and speak,
A twilight spun with violet dreams,
Cascades in rivers, in starlit streams.
The mountains, cloaked in amethyst haze,
Held secrets old as the ancient days.
Their ridges danced with a lavender glow,
Where spirits of dusk would ebb and flow.
Victoria, with her heart ablaze,
Lusted for Desi through fevered days.
Her longing burned like a comet's flight,
A reckless spark in the velvet night.
The heavens watched, their purple spun,
Threads of fate that could not be undone.
They saw her crave, her soul's desire,
A love that flared like a funeral pyre.
From misty heights, the spirits fell,
Draped in hues of a twilight spell.
The mountains' breath, a spectral wail,
Wove through the valleys, a ghostly trail.
They came for her, these purple shades,
Born of the heavens, where light degrades.
No longer bound to the starry dome,
They haunted the earth where her heart did roam.
"Victoria," they sang, in whispers cold,
"Your lust has torn what the heavens hold."
Their violet spins wrapped tight her soul,
A shroud of longing, no longer whole.
The Appalachian winds now moan her name,
Through purple crags where the shadows claim.
Her love for Desi, a fleeting fire,
Brought down the heavens, their wrath entire.
In moonlit hollows, the mountains weep,
Their purple secrets forever keep.

Victoria wanders, her heart's disgrace,
Haunted by spins of the heavens' embrace.

DEAD DREAMS-FORSAKEN DAYS

In the hollows where dead dreams decay,

Victoria perished in a lustful fray.

Her heart, consumed by Desi's flame,

Drew wrath from shadows that bore her name.

Rose and Charlotta Dee, with vengeful cries,

Unleashed their fury from spectral skies.

Their purple rage, a venomous stream,

Flowed from the mountains, a haunting dream.

The Appalachian peaks, in amethyst scorn,

Shook with anger, their ridges torn.

Their ancient breath, a chilling wail,

Cast her soul to the river's pale.

The river swelled, a mirror of spite,

Swallowing her in its murky night.

Townsfolk gathered, their voices grim,

Cursed her lust as the waters brim.

Dead dreams arose, forsaken days,

Wove her end in a twilight haze.

Rose and Charlotta, the mountains' might,

With river and folk, snuffed out her light.

In silence now, the hollows weep,

Where Victoria's ghost in shadows sleeps.

A tale of lust, by wrath undone,

Beneath the Appalachian sun.

PROPHECY

Beneath the purple Appalachian skies,
A flood arose with ancient cries.
The river swelled, a prophet's decree,
What the land binds, no soul sets free.
Victoria, with her lustful heart,
Sought to tear Desi's bond apart.
Against the earth's unyielding will,
She dared the flood, her fate to fill.
The waters rose, a spectral tide,
In prophecy's grip, where secrets hide.
The land's embrace, a sacred knot,
Held firm as her rebellion fought.
Spirits watched from misty heights,
Rose and Charlotta, guardians of night.
Their vengeance brewed in amethyst air,
A judgment born of silent prayer.
The flood consumed her, cold and deep,
A price for vows the land would keep.
No cry could save, no love could mend,
The prophecy claimed its bitter end.
In silence now, the spirits reign,
Their wrath a shroud of purple stain.
What the land binds, no heart may part,
Victoria's death seals the prophet's art.

TIME'S TRAGEDY

Beneath the Appalachian's purple veil,
Time's Tragedy weaves its mournful tale.
A clock ticks soft, yet loud with doom,
Where love and land seal Victoria's tomb.
The river rises, time's relentless hand,
Bound by mountains, an ancient land.
What fate has knit, no heart may sever,
A prophecy carved in time forever.
Rose and Charlotta, spirits of old,
Watch as her lust turns passion cold.
The flood consumes, a temporal tide,
Where seconds drown what dreams reside.
Each chime a chain, each hour a weight,
Time's Tragedy seals her fateful fate.
The land holds firm, its will unbowed,
In silence, time cries out aloud.
The dawn reveals a hollow stream,
Where time erased her fleeting dream.
Time's Tragedy, in purple skies,
Etches her end where no one cries.

DISTORTED

In the shadow of the Appalachians' ancient spine,
Where mist clings low and the stars refuse to shine,
The Cursed River snakes, a vein of whispered dread,
Its waters thick with secrets of the restless dead.
Charlotta Dee, the witch, with eyes like burning coal,
Wove spells in moonlit hollows, blessing hearts and souls.
Her voice, a chant that bent the roots of gnarled trees,
Summoned shades and cryptids, stirred by midnight's breeze.
Bigfoot's shadow lumbered, Mothman's wings did flare,
Aliens hummed in starships, their lights a sickly glare.
The townsfolk spoke her name in fear, their doors barred tight,
For Charlotta's magic twisted day into endless night.
Victoria, sweet Victoria, with love as fierce as flame,
Pined for Desi's laughter, his touch, his whispered name.
By the river's edge they'd meet, where willows softly wept,
But the Cursed River hungered, its promises unkept.
A flood roared down the mountains, a beast of froth and stone,
It swallowed Victoria whole, leaving her spirit lost, alone.
Her cries still echo faintly, where the waters churn and seethe,
A ghost bound to the river, her love a wound that breathes.
When Victoria died, they say the sky itself did scream,
Her blood soaked the earth, unraveling time's seam.
The river surged, the mountains groaned, the stars fell out of line,
And time itself grew warped, a knot of grief divine.

Hours stretched to centuries, then snapped to fleeting breaths,

The dead walked with the living, defying laws of death.

Victoria's shade holds all, though she's long since turned to dust,

Her love is a looping echo, caught in time's cruel rust.

The townsfolk haunt the hollows, their faces pale and drawn,

Whispering of lights in the sky that vanish come the dawn.

Cryptids stalk the ridges—Mothman, Wendigo, and more,

Their eyes like lanterns glowing, guarding secrets of the lore.

Aliens weave through treetops, their craft a silent hum,

While Charlotta's laughter lingers, a spell that won't succumb.

The river bends the seconds, folds years into a haze,

Each ripple traps a memory, each wave a ghostly maze.

In the Appalachians' cradle, where the Cursed River flows,

Time frays like tattered muslin, and no one truly knows

If today is now or then, if the dead outnumber life,

Or if the mountains' heart still beats with Charlotta's strife.

Victoria weeps for Desi, her voice a drowned refrain,

The cryptids howl, the aliens watch, the townsfolk bear the pain.

And through the mist, the river runs, its curse forever near,

Binding love, and death, and time, in the mountains' endless fear.

IMMORTALITY

In the Appalachians' ancient, weathered embrace,

Where peaks pierce the sky and shadows find their place,

The dead walk immortal, their footsteps soft as dust,

Bound to the mountains' heart, where time corrodes to rust.

No grave can hold them, no coffin seals their fate,

Their souls are stitched to the ridges, defying heaven's gate.

From Charlotta Dee, the witch, with her curses sharp as bone,

To Victoria's drowned lament, forever lost, alone—

Each spirit clings to the hollows, where the air is thick with dread,

Their whispers weave the fog, immortal, never truly dead.

The townsfolk linger, shades of flannel, grief, and toil,

Their eyes like lantern sparks, rooted deep in sacred soil.

Devils wanders, seeking Victoria, their love a wound unhealed,

Their hands graze in the mist, a bond that time's repealed.

Cryptids join the vigil—Mothman's wings, a mournful sweep,

Wendigos howl hunger, their cries too raw to sleep.

Aliens, otherworldly, drift through starless, tangled skies,

Their lights a fleeting pulse, where mortal reason dies.

Every soul, this world and beyond, is tethered to the stone,

The mountains' pulse a magnet, claiming flesh and bone.

From miners crushed in darkness to lovers torn by flood,

Their essence stains the rivers, their pain the ancient mud.

The Cursed River binds them, its waters black as fate,

A thread through every spirit, no matter love or hate.

Time twists, unravels, knots—yet none can ever flee,

The Appalachians cradle all, for all eternity.

Immortal dead, they roam where starlight fears to tread,

Their voices hum in treetops, their stories never said.

Otherworldly shades—beings from realms unseen—

Mingle with the mountain's ghosts in a timeless, haunted dream.

The peaks stand as sentinels, their roots a soulbound cage,

Each spirit trapped, yet endless, in an unyielding, deathless age.

So walk the trails with caution, where the air grows thin and cold,

For the Appalachians keep the souls—of worlds both young and old.

SHAPESHIFTER

In the Appalachians' gloom, where the Cursed River creeps,
Its waters hold the echoes of the secrets that it keeps.
Jimmy Charles, long drowned, in the flood's unyielding embrace,
Rises now, a shapeshifter, with a ever-changing face.
Centuries ago, the river stole his breath beneath its tide,
His body sank in darkness, where the mountain's spirits hide.
But death could not confine him; the peaks wove spells unseen,
And Jimmy woke, a phantom, in a form both fierce and lean.
He shifts—a bear with eyes like coals, then mist that twists and
sighs,
A crow with wings of shadow, slicing through the starless skies.
Now a man, now a stranger, his features blur and mend,
A creature born of river mud, where time and death transcend.
The Cursed River carved him, its currents gave him flight,
Each ripple shapes his essence, each wave ignites his sight.
He walks the fog-draped hollows, where cryptids softly tread,
His voice a haunting murmur, neither living nor quite dead.
No grave can chain his spirit, no flood can still his will,
He shifts through forms eternal, on ridge and shadowed hill.
The mountains pulse with power, their roots his endless throne,
Jimmy Charles, the shapeshifter, claimed by water, earth, and stone.
The river laughs, a serpent, its waters cold and sly,
Binding Jimmy's boundless soul beneath the mountain's eye.
He weaves through ancient forests, a fleeting, formless spark,
Forever bound, forever free, in the Appalachians' dark.

VIBRATIONS

The Appalachian Mountains loomed like silent sentinels, their peaks shrouded in a mist that clung like a second skin. Rose stood on the edge of the Cursed River, its waters sluggish and dark, murmuring secrets only the dead could decipher. The air was heavy with the scent of damp earth and pine, but beneath it, a pulse thrummed—an ancient rhythm that vibrated through the ground, the trees, and deep into her bones.

Rose pressed a hand to her swollen belly, feeling the life within her stir. Desi's child, their child, was due any day now, a spark of hope in a place where time twisted and the past refused to rest. But it wasn't just the baby's kicks that stirred her. For weeks, a strange vibration had hummed inside her, a low, resonant frequency that seemed to echo the mountains themselves. It wasn't painful, not exactly—just relentless, like a tuning fork struck deep in her core, resonating with something vast and unseen.

She'd felt it first on a night when the stars hid and the river seemed to hum louder than usual. She'd been lying beside Desi in their small cabin, his arm draped over her, his breath steady. That night, the vibrations began as a faint tremor in her chest, spreading like ripples across still water. At first, she thought it was the baby, but it was different—deeper, older, as if the mountains themselves were whispering through her.

Now, standing by the river, the vibrations were stronger, syncing with a pulse she felt rising from the earth. The Appalachians were alive, always had been, but something was shifting. The air crackled with a strange energy, and the trees seemed to lean closer, their branches trembling without wind. She'd heard and experienced the stories— Charlotta Dee, the witch whose curses still lingered; Jimmy Charles, the shapeshifter who'd drowned and risen as something else; the cryptids and alien lights that flickered in the hollows. The mountains were a crucible of the impossible, and now they were stirring, as if heralding something new.

Rose closed her eyes, letting the vibrations guide her senses. They weren't just in her body now; they were in the river's flow, the rustle of leaves, the distant howl of something not quite animal. It was as if the mountains were preparing, their ancient rhythm aligning with the life growing inside her. She felt a kick, sharp and insistent, and the vibrations surged, a warm hum that made her gasp. The baby knew. The baby was part of this, tied to the mountains' pulse, to the warped time that held the dead and the living in an endless dance.

She remembered the night she'd told Desi about the vibrations. They'd sat by the fire, the cabin creaking under the weight of the mountain's gaze. "It's like the earth is singing," she'd said, her voice barely above a whisper. Desi's eyes softened. "Maybe it's the mountains welcoming our kid," he'd said, his hand resting on her belly. But there was a question in his voice, a fear of this place where ghosts still lingered, where Jimmy Charles's shifting forms haunted the fog.

The townsfolk had noticed changes too. Old Man Carver swore the river's flow had reversed for a single night. Widow Hanks claimed the Mothman's eyes glowed brighter in the sky, watching the valley with purpose. Even the strange lights—those alien flickers that never quite explained themselves—had pulsed in patterns, as if signaling. Rose felt it all converging, the mountains' vibrations growing stronger, more urgent, like a heartbeat quickening before a birth.

One evening, as the sun bled red into the horizon, Rose wandered to the river's edge again. The vibrations were almost unbearable now, a symphony of energy that made her skin hum and her heart race. She knelt, pressing her hands to the damp earth, and felt it—the mountains' pulse, syncing perfectly with the rhythm in her womb. A vision flashed: a child, her child, with eyes like the river's depths, born under a sky where time unraveled. This child would carry the mountains' secrets, a bridge between the living, the dead, and the otherworldly that roamed these ridges. It would be a girl child with one clear sky blue eye like her mother and one brown eye like her father.

The contractions hit, sharp and real, pulling her back to the present. The vibrations peaked, a crescendo that shook the ground beneath her. The river seemed to roar, though its surface stayed calm. Somewhere in the distance, a cryptid's cry echoed, and a light pulsed in the sky. Rose gripped the earth, her breath ragged, knowing the time was near. The mountains were ready, and so was she.

Their child would be born soon, under the watchful eyes of the Appalachians, in a place where the dead walked and time bent. The vibrations sang of a new beginning, a soul tied to the river, the witch's curses, the shapeshifter's forms, and the alien lights. Rose stood, steady despite the pain, and whispered to the mountains, "We're ready." The pulse answered, strong and sure, heralding a birth that would echo through the ages.

DEATHLESS MUSIC

In the cradle of the Appalachians, where shadows weave with light,
The Cursed River hums a tune that blurs the day and night.
Rose's child was born at dawn, when mist gave way to flame,
A girl with one clear sky-blue eye, her mother's shining claim,
And one deep brown, like Desi's gaze, a father's quiet grace,
Her eyes a map of earth and stars, a bridge to time and space.
The mountains woke to greet her, their peaks aglow with sound,
A deathless music swelling, from roots deep in the ground.
The river sang, its waters clear, no longer cursed, but free,
Each ripple chanting hymns of life for this child's destiny.
The pines swayed soft, their needles tuned to whispers of the skies,
While cryptids paused in reverence, their calls like lullabies.
No witch's curse could silence it, no flood could drown its call,
The music wove through hollows, past the graves where spirits
    sprawl.
Jimmy Charles, the shapeshifter, took form as morning deer,
His eyes reflecting starlight, as the song grew sharp and clear.
The Mothman's wings fell silent, the alien lights aligned,
The universe itself expanded, its glory intertwined.
One blue eye caught the heavens, where the cosmos spun and
    gleamed,
One brown eye held the mountains, where the ancient dreams are
    dreamed.
The deathless music surged for her, a symphony unbound,
Each note a pulse of timeless love, in every stone and sound.

The river's voice grew golden, the ridges' chant took flight,

A melody of endless life beneath the starlit night.

The Appalachians sang her name, their voices fierce and true,

The sky unfurled in colors vast—red, gold, and endless blue.

For Rose's child, the world remade, its glory hers to claim,

A girl of dual-hued eyes, born to carry love's bright flame.

The deathless music lingers still, in streams and peaks it flows,

A song for her, eternal, where the universe still grows.

BLACK RAIN

Beneath the Appalachians' watchful peaks, where shadows twist and
   sway,
The black rain falls in solemn sheets, a shroud for break of day.
The Cursed River murmurs low, its waters dark and deep,
As Rose brings forth her infant girl, where ancient spirits weep.
Lucinda Blue, the child's named, for eyes that hold the sky,
One blue as Rose's boundless gaze, one brown where Desi's lie.
The baptism waits by river's edge, where willows bend and sigh,
The black rain weaves a sacred veil beneath a starless sky.
No preacher speaks, no church bells toll, the mountains are the choir,
Their vibrations hum through earth and bone, a pulse of primal fire.
The townsfolk gather, silent, awed, their faces pale as bone,
For Lucinda's rite is woven with the river's undertone.
The black rain falls, like tears of gods, each drop a whispered vow,
It kisses Lucinda's tiny brow, anointing her somehow.
Rose lifts her high, the water cold, the river's touch a blade,
Yet warm with love, it claims the child, as curses seem to fade.
"Lucinda Blue," the mother chants, her voice a steady flame,
The name resounds through hollows vast, forever staking claim.
The rain's dark song entwines with hers, a hymn both fierce and
   true,
The mountains echo back the call, their notes as black as dew.
No cryptid stirs, no alien light dares pierce this holy hour,
The black rain holds its own strange grace, a consecrating power.
The river swirls, its depths alive, reflecting Lucinda's eyes,
One blue for hope, one brown for earth, beneath the endless skies.
The baptism seals her to this place, where time and death entwine,
Lucinda Blue, of rain and ridge, a spark of the divine.
The black rain falls, its music vast, a blessing wild and free,
For her, the child of river's heart, eternal as the sea.

HUMAN SLEEP

In the Appalachian cradle, where the night is soft and deep,
Lucinda Blue, the infant star, lies wrapped in gentle sleep.
Her sky-blue eye, like Rose's, dreams of heavens yet unseen,
Her brown eye, Desi's quiet earth, holds forests calm and green.
The black rain's hymn has faded, though its echo lingers still,
A whisper in the river's flow, a sigh on every hill.
The mountains hum a lullaby, their ancient voices low,
Their vibrations weave a blanket, where peaceful slumbers grow.
Lucinda Blue, so small, so new, her breath a tender rhyme,
Sleeps beautiful, untouched by grief, unmarred by twisted time.
No cryptid's cry disturbs her rest, no alien light intrudes,
The Cursed River guards her dreams with gentle, lapping moods.
Her tiny hands curl soft as ferns, her cheeks like moonlit dew,
Each sigh a note of innocence, each dream a world anew.
The hollows hold their breath for her, the ridges softly sway,
Their deathless song a cradle now, to keep the dark at bay.
No witch's curse, no restless dead, can pierce this sacred calm,
Her human heart beats steady, warm, a quiet, living psalm.
Lucinda Blue, in slumber's grace, is beauty's purest bloom,
A starlit child of mountain and rain, asleep in love's perfume.
The universe expands for her, its glory soft and near,
Each twinkling star a whispered wish, each dream a love sincere.
In peaceful rest, she shines, serene, beneath the Appalachian sky,
Lucinda Blue, forever home, where sweetest dreams don't die.

THE WATCHMAN

In the Appalachian night, where shadows twist and creep,
The Watchman stands, unyielding, o'er Lucinda Blue's sweet sleep.
No name he claims, no face he shows, a sentinel of stone,
His presence carved in starless dark, where ancient winds have
blown.
By the Cursed River's edge he looms, where black rain softly falls,
His silent gaze a fortress, guarding Lucinda's tender calls.
Her sky-blue eye, her earthen brown, rest peaceful in her dreams,
While he, the Watchman, holds the line where time unravels seams.
No cryptid dares to cross his path, no Mothman's wings take flight,
The alien lights grow dim and still beneath his boundless sight.
Charlotta's curses falter here, her spells dissolve in air,
For the Watchman's vigil knows no end, his will a steadfast prayer.
The mountains hum their ancient song, their pulse his steady beat,
Each ridge and hollow bends to him, where earth and ether meet.
He wards the shades of restless dead, keeps Jimmy's shifting form at
bay,
Ensuring Lucinda's gentle rest remains till break of day.
No sword he wields, no voice he speaks, yet power thrums within,
A guardian born of river's depths, of rock, of root, of kin.
The black rain whispers secrets old, but heeds his silent call,
Its drops anoint the sacred ground where Lucinda's dreams don't
fall.
Through warped and tangled threads of time, his watch will never
cease,

For Lucinda Blue, the starlit child, he carves a space of peace.

The Watchman stands, eternal, still, beneath the starless blue,

His heart the mountains' endless vow, to guard sweet Lucinda Blue.

INTERRUPTED CRY

In the Appalachian night, where darkness drinks the stars,

Lucinda Blue awakes with cries that pierce the midnight's scars.

Her wails, a jagged symphony, unravel sleep's thin thread,

A colic's grip, relentless, in her cradle's lonely bed.

The cabin trembles with her voice, a storm of infant pain,

The Cursed River echoes back, its ripples thick with rain.

Rose stirs, her heart a knotted ache, Desi's eyes grow wide,

Their baby's sobs a blade that cuts where love and fear collide.

No lullaby can soothe her, no touch can ease her plight,

Her sky-blue eye and earthen brown are drowned in endless night.

The mountains hum, uneasy, their pulse a troubled beat,

As Lucinda's cries climb higher, no respite, no retreat.

Then through the dark, a shadow shifts, a whisper soft as dew,

Charlotta Dee, the witch of old, steps silent into view.

No curse upon her lips tonight, no malice in her gaze,

Her spirit glows with tender light, through the cabin's moonless

    haze.

Rose feels a chill, a knowing spark, Desi's breath grows still,

The air is thick with ancient love, a warmth no night can kill.

Charlotta kneels by Lucinda's side, her hands of mist and grace,

She hums a song of starlit streams, a balm for time and space.

The baby's cries grow softer now, her sobs begin to fade,

As Charlotta's spectral fingers weave a spell of love remade.

No colic's claw can linger here, no pain can hold its claim,

The witch's voice, a mother's croon, dissolves the hurt, the shame.

Lucinda sees her, eyes wide bright—one blue, one brown, aglow,

The spirit's love a river deep, where only healing flows.

Rose clutches Desi's hand, their hearts alight with quiet awe,

They sense her there, the witch's care, in every breath they draw.

The mountains sigh, the river calms, the night grows soft and clear,

Charlotta's presence lingers, though her form begins to shear.

Lucinda Blue, now hushed, now still, drifts back to gentle rest,

Her tiny chest rises slow, by love's old magic blessed.

The Watchman nods from shadowed peaks, the black rain hums its
tune,

Charlotta fades, her work complete, beneath the unseen moon.

Rose and Desi hold their child, their fears now laid to sleep,

For Lucinda Blue is whole again, in love's eternal keep.

SACRIFICE

In the Appalachians' ancient arms, where time and shadow blend,
Lucinda Blue grows wild and free, where rivers twist and bend.
Her sky-blue eye catches dawn's first spark, her brown eye holds the
    earth,
A child of mountain, rain, and star, she blooms with boundless
    worth.
The mountains, old as memory, their peaks a jagged crown,
Give up their secrets, soft and slow, to let her spirit roam.
They quiet their vibrations, hush their pulse of endless years,
To carve a path for Lucinda, free from grief, from ancient fears.
The Cursed River, once a snare for souls like Victoria's shade,
Softens its relentless current, lets its curses gently fade.
It offers her its gleaming depths, a mirror for her dreams,
Its waters part to set her free, unbinding tangled streams.
The cryptids—Mothman, Wendigo—step back from moonlit trails,
Their eyes, once fierce, now sentinel, guard where her courage sails.
Jimmy Charles, the shapeshifter, weaves forms of light, not dread,
His fleeting shapes a playful dance to guide her steps ahead.
The townsfolk, bound by haunted pasts, their whispers worn and
    thin,
Release their tales of Charlotta's curse, let go their fear of sin.
They offer Lucinda smiles and songs, their hands unclenched,
    unbowed,
Sacrificing years of doubt to see her spirit proud.
The alien lights that pulse above, in skies no star can claim,

Dim their glow to let her run, un tethered by their flame.

The Watchman, silent, yields his post, his vigil soft and still,

Allowing Lucinda's heart to soar beyond the ridge and hill.

The black rain falls, but gently now, a blessing, not a chain,

Each drop a vow to set her free from sorrow's lingering stain.

The mountains give their granite strength, the river gives its flow,

The creatures lend their wildness, so her spirit learns to grow.

No witch's spell, no ghostly wail, no twisted time can hold,

Lucinda Blue, with eyes of earth and sky, grows fierce and bold.

The Appalachians' sacrifice, their gift of boundless grace,

Frees her to dance through life unbound, a star in time's vast space.

She runs through hollows, laughs with streams, her spirit light and
    free,

A child of all, yet owned by none, as wild as wild can be.

The mountains, rivers, creatures, folk—they gave their all, it's true,

To let the world embrace the fire of radiant Lucinda Blue.

DOMINION

In her twenties, Lucinda Blue, with eyes of sky and earth,
Stands where the Appalachians hum, their pulse her heart's own
    birth.
Her sky-blue gaze holds starlit dreams, her brown eye roots her
    deep,
Yet the call of New York City stirs her soul from mountain sleep.
She whispers farewells to the peaks, their granite strength her guide,
To the Cursed River's gleaming flow, where secrets still reside.
The spirits—Charlotta's ghostly glow—offer sighs of tender care,
While cryptids, Mothman, Wendigo, watch silent in the air.
The alien lights pulse one last time, a farewell soft and strange,
Her parents, Rose and Desi, weep, their love too vast to change.
Grandparents, etched by mountain years, press blessings to her
    hands,
Their tears a map to call her back to these eternal lands.
"I'll rule the world," she vows aloud, her spirit fierce and free,
Seeking dominion over life, where power's meant to be.
The city's gleam, its towering spires, beckon with a roar,
And Lucinda leaves the hollows, chasing dreams of something more.
In New York's pulse, she finds a man, his face a chiseled art,
His charm a snare, his voice a chain that binds her reckless heart.
She loves him deep, but love turns sharp, a blade beneath his grin,
He rules her with a crueler hand, his dominance a sin.
His fists, his words, they bruise her soul, her body bears the cost,
This devil with a pretty face, her freedom cruelly lost.

She named him so, this shadowed man, who dims her radiant light,

His love a cage, his rage a storm that haunts her in the night.

Yet Lucinda's spirit, mountain-born, cannot be bound for long,

Her eyes—blue sky, brown earth—recall the river's ancient song.

One moonless night, she breaks away, her heart a beating drum,

Fleeing the devil's brutal grip, to where her soul came from.

The Appalachians call her back, their ridges stark and true,

The river hums, the spirits sigh, "Return, sweet Lucinda Blue."

The cryptids stalk the shadowed paths, their eyes a guiding flame,

The alien lights weave through the sky, whispering her name.

Her parents wait, their arms outstretched, grandparents' prayers a
   shield,

The mountains part their ancient heart to let her wounds be healed.

But he pursues, the devil-man, his pretty face a mask,

His rage a storm that hunts her through the wilds, a brutal task.

Into the mountains' embrace she runs, where time and spirits blend,

Lucinda Blue, unbound once more, her freedom to defend.

The peaks close ranks, the river roars, the cryptids guard her flight,

The devil chases, lost in mist, consumed by endless night.

TEARS AND SEPULCHRE

The Appalachians loomed, their peaks shrouded in a mist that clung like a warning. The Cursed River snaked through the hollows, its waters whispering of ancient grief, while the air pulsed with the restless hum of the mountains. Lucinda Blue had fled New York City, her heart battered but unbroken, escaping the man she called the Devil with a Pretty Face. His name, once sweet on her lips, now tasted of ash—his charm a mask for cruelty, his hands quick to bruise her body and soul. She'd run back to her roots, to the mountains, the river, and the spirits that cradled her childhood, hoping their embrace could shield her. But he followed, relentless, a predator drawn by her light.

He stalked her through the ridges, his boots silent on the moss, his eyes gleaming with a hunger that no mountain could sate. The townsfolk of the small Appalachian settlement, weathered by years of hauntings and hard living, saw him first at dusk, his face too perfect, like a statue carved from deceit. He moved among them, his voice smooth as river stones, but his threats were sharp as thorns. He cornered Old Man Carver by the general store, demanding Lucinda's whereabouts, his fist splitting the old man's lip when answers came too slow. Widow Hanks, who'd seen Mothman's eyes in the sky, tried to defy him, but a single blow sent her sprawling, her warnings drowned in fear.

Rose and Desi, Lucinda's parents, felt his shadow fall over their cabin. He stood at their door, his smile a blade, demanding their daughter.

"She's mine," he said, his voice a low growl, his fist splintering the doorframe when Rose spat defiance. Desi's hands trembled, his love for Lucinda warring with the terror of this man who seemed untouchable, his cruelty a force no human strength could match. Lucinda's grandparents, their faces etched with mountain years, prayed by the fire, their voices quaking as they begged the spirits for protection. But the Devil with a Pretty Face only laughed, his presence a stain on their sacred ground.

Lucinda hid by the Cursed River, her sky-blue eye and earthen brown reflecting the water's restless churn. She felt him near, his steps a drumbeat in her chest, his gaze a weight that pressed her breath thin. The mountains tried to shield her, their vibrations rising in a protective hum, but he walked through their song unscathed. The river surged, its currents swirling with the fury of the dead, yet he waded its shallows, his boots untouched by its pull. The cryptids—Mothman's wings slicing the air, Wendigo's howl echoing from the ridges—circled close, their eyes glowing with primal rage, but he brushed past them, his pretty face unmarred, his cruelty a shield no claw could pierce.

The alien lights pulsed in the sky, their strange patterns flashing warnings, but he ignored their glow, his focus locked on Lucinda. The spirits of the dead, those bound to the mountains' timeless warp, moaned in the fog, their whispers urging her to run. Yet he tracked her through the hollows, his steps unerring, his laughter a cold blade cutting through their cries.

One night, as Lucinda crouched in a grove of twisted pines, Charlotta Dee appeared, her spectral form shimmering with starlight tears. The witch's eyes, once fierce with curses, now brimmed with sorrow. "Child," she whispered, her voice a trembling thread, "his evil runs deeper than my spells can reach. I cannot stop him, not yet." Lucinda, her heart pounding, touched the ghost's translucent hand, feeling love in Charlotta's grief, but no power to end her flight. The witch faded, her tears mingling with the black rain that fell, unable to break the Devil's pursuit.

Jimmy Charles, the shapeshifter, rose from the river's edge, his form rippling—now a wolf, now a bear, now a man with eyes of fire. He'd heard Lucinda's cries, felt her fear through the mountains' pulse. He lunged at the Devil, shifting mid-stride into a panther, claws slashing for the man's perfect face. But the Devil only smiled, his hand catching Jimmy's throat, tossing him aside like a rag. Jimmy tried again, becoming a hawk, talons aimed at eyes, then a stag, antlers lowered to charge. Each time, the Devil stood untouched, his laughter mocking the shapeshifter's desperate dance. "You're nothing," he sneered, his voice a venom that burned the air.

Through the town, he left a trail of fear—broken doors, bruised faces, silenced prayers. The townsfolk cowered, their stories of cryptids and spirits no match for his brutality. Lucinda's parents clung to hope, her grandparents to faith, but the Devil's presence was a storm that bent even the strongest will. He found Lucinda at dawn, by the river's bend, her breath a fog in the chill. "You can't run," he said, his pretty face a cruel promise, his hand raised to claim her again.

The mountains roared, their vibrations a futile cry. The river churned, the spirits wailed, the cryptids howled, and the alien lights flickered in despair. Jimmy Charles, battered but unyielding, shifted once more, a shadow of himself, but the Devil's power held. Not even Charlotta's ghostly love could break his stride. The dead, the creatures, the mountains themselves—they fought for Lucinda Blue, but his evil was a force too vast, too dark, not yet undone.

Lucinda stood, her eyes blazing—one sky, one earth—her spirit unbroken. She ran again, deeper into the mountains, knowing the fight wasn't over. The Devil with a Pretty Face followed, his steps a relentless drum, but the Appalachians whispered a promise: not yet, but soon, her freedom would come.

In the Appalachian night, where mists and shadows blend,
Lucinda Blue flees through the peaks, her heart too bruised to mend.
Tears fall like black rain, heavy with her pain and fear,
Each drop a silent requiem for dreams that disappear.
The sepulchre of mountains looms, a tomb of ancient stone,
Its hollows cradle grief and ghosts, where lost souls roam alone.
Her sky-blue eye weeps oceans, her brown eye holds the earth,
Tears carve rivers down her cheeks, a map of shattered worth.
The Cursed River mirrors them, its waters dark and deep,
A liquid crypt that drinks her sorrow, where the dead still softly
    weep.
The sepulchre of ridges stands, eternal, cold, and vast,
Each tear a prayer for freedom from the Devil's brutal past.
Charlotta Dee appears once more, her spirit cloaked in woe,
Her own tears gleam like starlight, falling soft as mountain snow.
"Child," she whispers, voice a thread, frayed by love and loss,
"My spells can't break his pretty mask, nor lift your heavy cross."
The sepulchre of hollows sighs, its granite heart her tomb,
Yet holds her tears like sacred wine within its shadowed womb.
Jimmy Charles, the shapeshifter, shifts through forms in vain,
His eyes, too, brim with spectral tears, reflecting Lucinda's pain.
He fights the Devil with a Pretty Face, whose cruelty knows no end,
But tears and claws can't pierce his will, nor make his malice bend.
The sepulchre of ancient pines, their roots a tangled grave,
Collects the tears of man and beast, yet none her soul can save.
The townsfolk weep in silence, their faces bruised and worn,
Their tears a stream of quiet grief for Lucinda, lost, forlorn.
Rose and Desi, parents bound by love, shed rivers of despair,
Their grandparents' ancient eyes spill sorrow through the air.
The sepulchre of memory holds their tears like sacred trust,
Each drop a vow to shield her, though their hopes have turned to
    dust.
The cryptids mourn, their cries a dirge—Mothman's wings grow
    still,
The Wendigo's howl a sob that echoes from the hill.
Alien lights pulse faintly, tears of starlight in their glow,
Yet the Devil stalks unyielding, where their cosmic rivers flow.

The sepulchre of starless skies, a vault of endless night,
Entombs their grief, their fleeting hope, in beams of fading light.
Lucinda's tears, a torrent now, carve paths through dirt and stone,
Each one a fleeting sepulchre for dreams she'll never own.
The mountains, river, spirits, dead—they weep with her as one,
Their sorrow builds a fragile shield, though freedom's yet unwon.
The Devil with a Pretty Face pursues, his laughter cold as death,
His shadow taints the tear-soaked ground, defying every breath.
Yet in the sepulchre of tears, where grief and granite meet,
Lucinda's spirit burns alive, her heart too strong to cheat.
The mountains hold her weeping, the river sings her pain,
Each tear a seed of reckoning, to bloom through blackest rain.
The sepulchre of Appalachia waits, its depths a patient vow,
For Lucinda Blue will rise again—her tears will show her how.

BOUNTY FOR THE DECEASED

The Appalachian night hung heavy, the air thick with the scent of black rain and the Cursed River's restless churn. Lucinda Blue crouched in a hollow, her sky-blue eye and earthen brown reflecting the flicker of distant alien lights. Her breath was ragged, her body bruised from the Devil with a Pretty Face, the man who'd stalked her from New York City back to these haunted mountains. His cruelty had scarred her, his fists a brutal hymn, but her spirit, forged in the ridges' ancient pulse, burned unyielding.

The town had a new preacher, Finn McGraw, a gaunt man with eyes like burning coal and a voice that carried the weight of divine wrath. A staunch man of God, Rev. Finn wielded the power of exorcism, his faith a blade honed by years of battling unseen evils. He'd heard the whispers of Lucinda's plight, the townsfolk's fear, the bruises on Old Man Carver and Widow Hanks, and the splintered door of Rose and Desi's cabin. The Devil with a Pretty Face had terrorized them all, his charm a venom that no cryptid's claw or spirit's wail could pierce.

Finn stood in the town square, his Bible raised like a shield, the wind howling as if the mountains themselves leaned in to listen. "This man, this devil," he thundered, his voice cutting through the mist, "is a blight upon God's earth. I name him a bounty for the deceased, a curse to be undone!" The townsfolk, gathered in trembling silence, felt the air shift, the river's hum grow fierce. The dead, restless in their timeless sepulchre, stirred at his words, their whispers joining the preacher's c chant. Charlotta Dee's spirit flickered at the edge of the crowd, her tear-streaked face nodding in solemn accord.

The Devil with a Pretty Face laughed, his perfect features untouched by the preacher's fire. He stood by the river, unafraid, his eyes locked on Lucinda, who hid nearby, her heart pounding with both fear and resolve. Rev. Finn raised a cross, his voice rising in an exorcist's cadence, ancient words that burned the air. "By the power of the Almighty, I bind thee, foul spirit!" The mountains quaked, the river surged, and the cryptids—Mothman, Wendigo—howled in the shadows. Alien lights pulsed erratically, as if the cosmos itself recoiled. Yet the Devil stood unscathed, his laughter a blade that mocked the divine.

Jimmy Charles, the shapeshifter, tried once more, his form rippling into a bear, then a wolf, claws slashing at the Devil's chest. But the man's cruelty was a shield, his pretty face unmarred, his strength unholy. Lucinda watched, her tears falling like black rain, her spirit kindled by Charlotta's weeping presence. "You are enough," Charlotta's ghost whispered, her voice a thread of love. "You carry the mountains' heart." Lucinda's resolve hardened, her hand closing around a jagged stone from the river's edge.

The town's lawmen—Sheriff Tate and his deputy, Jeb, grizzled men who'd seen the mountains' strangest truths—had watched the Devil's terror unfold. They'd seen the bruises, heard the threats, felt the fear that gripped Rose, Desi, and Lucinda's grandparents. When Elias called a meeting in the shadowed church, they pledged their loyalty—not to the law of man, but to the justice of the mountains. "He ain't human," Tate muttered, his hand on his revolver. "And Lucinda's one of ours." The final confrontation came at midnight, under a sky where no stars dared shine. The Devil cornered Lucinda by the Cursed River, his hand raised to strike, his voice dripping venom. "You'll never leave me," he snarled, his pretty face a mask of rage. But Lucinda, her eyes blazing—one sky, one earth—swung the river stone with all the strength of her mountain-born soul. It struck his temple, and he staggered, blood marring his perfect features. She struck again, and again, her tears mingling with the black rain, her cries echoing the river's roar. The Devil with a Pretty Face fell, his body crumpling into the shallows, the river claiming his lifeless form.

The mountains went silent, their vibrations stilled. The cryptids retreated, their eyes glowing with quiet approval. The alien lights dimmed, as if turning away. Charlotta's spirit sighed, her form fading into the mist. Jimmy Charles, in human guise, stood watch, his gaze soft with pride. The dead, their whispers now a hymn, seemed to nod in the shadows.

Sheriff Tate and Jeb arrived, their lanterns casting long shadows. They saw Lucinda, trembling, the stone still in her hand, the Devil's body at her feet. Rev. Finn joined them, his Bible closed, his eyes fierce but kind. "It's done," he said, his voice a vow. Rose and Desi ran to their daughter, their arms a fortress, while her grandparents whispered prayers of thanks. The townsfolk, summoned by the river's strange calm, gathered in silence, their faces etched with relief and resolve. No one spoke of justice in the way of courts or men. The mountains, the river, the cryptids, the aliens, the dead—they all bore witness, and they all agreed. The Devil with a Pretty Face was a blight, and Lucinda Blue had purged him. Tate and Jeb dragged the body deep into the hollows, where the earth swallowed it whole, the river washing away the blood. The townsfolk swore silence, their loyalty to Lucinda a sacred bond. Rev. Finn blessed the ground, his exorcist's power sealing the act in divine secrecy.

The mountains kept her secret, their ridges closing ranks. The river sang a softer song, its curse now cleansed by grace. The cryptids and aliens faded into the night, their watch complete. The dead, from Charlotta to Victoria, hummed a quiet peace. Lucinda Blue stood tall, her spirit free, her heart reclaimed. Good had prevailed, not through force alone, but through the love that bound them all—preacher, lawmen, townsfolk, spirits, and the wild heart of the Appalachians.

No one spoke of the Devil's end. They rebuilt their doors, tended their bruises, and lifted Lucinda up as their own. She was their daughter, their fighter, their light. And in the silence of the mountains, her secret was kept, hidden forever in the sepulchre of stone and rain.

In the Appalachian cradle, where the mountains touch the sky,
Lucinda Blue stands resolute, her eyes of earth and high.
One blue as boundless heavens, one brown as sacred ground,
She seeks a covenant with God, where free will's grace is found.
The Cursed River whispers low, its waters dark with time,
The ridges hum of ancient vows, of love and loss sublime.
No cryptid's cry, no spirit's wail, no alien light's cold gleam,
Can bind her soul, for she was born to chase a boundless dream.
With God she makes her sacred pact, beneath the black rain's fall,
A promise carved in starlight, answering her spirit's call.
"I'll walk your path," she softly swears, "but let my heart be free,
To choose the road, to bear the weight, of all you've given me."
The mountains bow, their granite hearts acknowledge her bold plea,
The river sighs, its currents part, to let her will run free.
Charlotta Dee, with ghostly tears, bestows a tender smile,
Her spirit knows the strength it takes to walk that holy mile.
The Watchman, silent, nods his grace, his vigil soft and still,
The cryptids fade, their eyes aglow, respecting her fierce will.
The townsfolk, bruised by battles past, lift prayers to the divine,
For Lucinda's covenant with God, where freedom's roots entwine.
No devil's face, no matter how fair, can chain her soul again,
Her will, a flame that burns through fear, through sorrow, loss, and
    pain.
The aliens' lights pulse once, then dim, as if to mark her choice,
The dead, from graves of timeless earth, add whispers to her voice.
God's covenant, a living bond, does not demand her chains,
But offers strength to carve her path through joy and bitter pains.
Free will, her sacred birthright, shines brighter than the sun,
A gift to wield, a fire to hold, till all her days are done.
Lucinda Blue, with eyes of sky and earth, walks bold and free,
Her covenant with God a song of love and liberty.
The mountains, river, spirits, stars—they guard her chosen way,
For in her heart, free will and faith unite to greet the day.

THE END

I would like to thank my publisher Dustin Pickering for his support, advice, and for his friendship and professionalism.

Thank you to Nathan P. Khanna for the cover art and interior photos.

This book is dedicated to all of the powers of good that triumph daily over the powers of evil.

Amen!

www.ingramcontent.com/pod-product-compliance
Lightning Source LLC
Chambersburg PA
CBHW060358090426
42734CB00011B/2172